Anonymous

**The Old Fashion Farmer's Motives for Leaving the Church of England**

And Embracing the Roman Catholic Faith, and his Reasons...

Anonymous

**The Old Fashion Farmer's Motives for Leaving the Church of England**
*And Embracing the Roman Catholic Faith, and his Reasons...*

ISBN/EAN: 9783744773966

Printed in Europe, USA, Canada, Australia, Japan

Cover: Foto ©Lupo / pixelio.de

More available books at **www.hansebooks.com**

# THE
## Old Fashion FARMER's
# MOTIVES

FOR LEAVING THE

CHURCH of ENGLAND,

AND EMBRACING THE

Roman Catholic FAITH, &c.

# THE Old Fashion FARMER's MOTIVES FOR LEAVING THE CHURCH of ENGLAND, AND EMBRACING THE Roman Catholic FAITH;

AND HIS

Reasons for adhering to the same:

TOGETHER WITH AN

Explanation of some particular Points, misrepresented by those of a different Persuasion;

With an APPENDIX, by Way of Antidote against all upstart New Faiths:

Concluded with asking Thirty plain Questions.

Printed in the YEAR M,DCC,LXXVIII.

# ADVERTISEMENT.

## TO THE

# PUBLIC.

AS it is some years since I wrote the following sheets, it will be necessary to tell the reasons why they did not appear sooner, and what has occasioned their being published at this time.

And first, my reason for not publishing sooner, was owing to many of my friends being afraid that I should give offence; therefore, in condescension to them, I postponed it.

And my reasons for now presenting this to the Public, are first, to pre-

prevent people from being imposed upon by false notions concerning my conversion. Secondly, to shew that I became a Roman Catholic upon no other motive than from a thorough conviction of the truth of what that Church teaches; and that after a mature deliberation, and strict scrutiny into the most substantial points of her doctrine, especially those that seem to clash most *with sense, and man's natural inclination*, and not from any *particular pique*, or temporal interest. And, thirdly, to make it appear that Roman Catholics are by no means such abominable, idolatrous, wicked wretches, as some roaring Protestant preachers, and authors, represent them. Therefore I hope no one will think that I write with a design to vilify any Religion, but only to vindicate and clear the
Roman

Roman Catholic faith from the aspersions of all those who impose upon the ignorant, *by slander and misrepresentation*. As to the lowness of the style, and want of many other qualifications which make an author admired, I trust the candid Reader will excuse; because I profess myself no scholar, but only a Novice in writing, as well as in Religion. I confess that the greatest part of what I have wrote in defence of the holy Catholic faith, is what I have collected from the best authors I could meet with; and although I have not specified from whence I have had many of the passages which I have made use of, yet I hope this general declaration may acquit me of the charge of Plagiarism.

I would not have it imagined that I have the vanity to commence author

thor upon the suppofition of being able to convert or reclaim Proteftants; no, I too well know their obftinacy! If I can but undeceive, that is the higheft of my expectations, who am

*The Public's well-wifher*,

THE OLD FASHION FARMER.

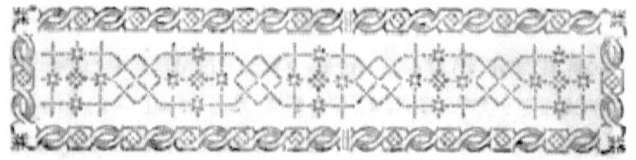

# THE
## Old Fashion FARMER's
# MOTIVES, &c.

THE first thing, that ever gave me uneasiness, concerning religion, was, to the best of my remembrance, receiving the Sacrament in the Church of England; for I thought there was not that reverence paid to it, as I judged it worthy of. I ever looked upon it as something more than a symbol of remembrance; and when I approached the altar, I came with great fear and respect: and at last began to think, that Christ must be really present, and that I ought to partake of his real body, and not in figure only. But as I could not demonstrate this to myself, I applied to an honest Parson for advice, and asked him, what it was that I received, when I took the sacrament? He told me bread and wine. I enquired farther, whether it was not something more than bread and wine? Upon which he gave me an answer no way to my satisfaction;

and upon that, I was determined never to receive any more in the Church of England.—Some time after this, I had a dispute with a Roman Catholic, about the word *Catholic*; which I endeavoured to prove in behalf of the Church of England: and on my insisting, that I was a Catholic, as being a member of the Church of England, he contradicted me, and affirmed, that it was plain, that the Church of England could not be the Holy Chatholic Church, which the creeds direct us to believe, because they were made many hundred years before the Protestant Church of England had either name or being. But as he found he could not prevail over me by dint of argument, he, at the same time, kindly advised me to look into the history of the times of the reformation, and examine when, and how, that extraordinary event happened: and he furthermore told me, to make a diligent search after the characters of those men who called themselves Reformers, and afterwards give him my opinion. Upon this, I set myself in earnest to read History; and for that purpose, borrowed *Guthrie*'s History of *England*, who is an approved author, and no small enemy to Popery; and I also looked over some other authors: and as I read the lives of Henry VIII, Edward VI, Q. Mary, and Q. Elizabeth, I made particular remarks, in

order

order to enable me to overcome all Papists for the future; but when I had finished writing them all out, and read them leisurely over, I was greatly surprized to find them run in favour of those very Papists, whom I had took so much pains to confute. For I could easily observe, from the remarks that I had made, that King Henry VIII, was the man who made the first great breach in the Church, especially here in England. And I further found, that he was moved thereunto, *not with a desire of reforming mankind, and making them more virtuous and good, but by a wicked and lustful desire, in order to obtain the greater liberty of indulging his inordinate and wicked appetites, in enjoying all the women he liked, and what money he wanted.* For which reasons I perceived, that he threw off the Pope's Supremacy, and abolished and plundered religious houses. By doing the first, he gained the liberty of divorcing his lawful and virtuous wife Catharine; and by the last, he got an abundance of money, by sacrilegiously robbing those holy places, which the piety of many great and good men had enriched, in order to maintain those that were poor; and them who sequestered themselves from the cares of the world, by dedicating their time and service to the almighty Maker of heaven and earth.

Now when I had read that King Henry did these deeds, I could not conceive that they were dictated unto him by the Holy Ghost, but rather *by the counsel and advice of some evil Genius, which was hurrying him on to fill up the measure of his iniquity.* I also found, that pride (which was the fall of Satan) was a great ingredient, which hastened on this sudden revolution. For I saw, that the King could not think himself happy whilst there was one on earth whom he might acknowledge his superior, (especially in spiritual affairs) because this superior, who was stiled the Father of the Church, *(for that is the signification of the word Pope)* would not wink at his wickedness, nor confirm his divorce, without his shewing just reasons why he sued for it: neither would he suffer him to commit adultery, without controul: all which lay heavy upon the King's proud and lustful soul; therefore, in order to strengthen himself against the Pope, he set about to distribute the riches of the religious houses amongst the nobility, and members of parliament, to involve them in the same guilt which he had took upon himself. And this I found he did by the advice of one Cromwell, whom King Henry afterwards made a Lord; *and for the great aptness that he had in villainy and hypocrisy, made and appointed him Inspector General, to enquire into the*

*the abuses (as they then termed it) of religious houses.* Which office he so well filled according to his master's desire, that I shall only say, the ruins we see at present of those places formerly dedicated to the service of God, and the relief of the poor, are sufficient marks for any one to judge of the vile intention of this promoter of sacrilege. But I further observed, that the fall of Cromwell was what ought to deter every other from the like offence; for in history I saw, *that the pit which he had dug for another, he fell into the midst of it himself*; the Almighty so disposing it, that he was the first who fell a sacrifice to that very law which he had got made to destroy one who opposed him; which law was namely this, " *That it should not* " *be necessary for any one that was tryed, to* " *be confronted with his witnesses.*" From this I learnt, *that verily there is a reward for the righteous; and that doubtless there are sore and grievous punishments for all those who set themselves to work wickedness, and to alter the ancient religion.*

Next I remarked, that King Edward VI. who established the Church of England, was not of years to discern truth from error, being scarce ten years of age when he began the Reformation; in which I saw he was directed by men of the most vicious inclinations, whose chief design was to enrich themselves

selves by *sacrilegious rapine*; who, in order to compass their wicked design, set about destroying and plundering all those religious places which had escaped the rapacious hands of King Henry, and his ministers: yea, and so impiously wicked were these men, that they robbed and plundered every church in the kingdom, of all its most costly ornaments. This proved it very plain to me, that *plunder* was the grand design of the first Reformers *(or rather Deformers)* of religion. And when I came to view the Transactions of the next reign, I was fully satisfied, that *a Reformation of Religion*, was the least that these men aimed at; for when Queen Mary ascended the throne, the most stiff *Protestants* under Edward, became now the most rigid *Catholics*; at the same time owning, that what they did before, was by their being led by the spirit of *ambition and avarice*, and not out of any motive to serve God more righteously and justly than heretofore. All which, I thought convincing enough to any reasonable and thinking mind, to make him forsake those paths *which these time-servers had chalked out*.

As a proof of what I have advanced, concerning the Reformers under King Edward, observe, that Archbishop Cranmer, who was the chief contriver of the Faith and Articles of the Church of England, did, in the reign of of Queen Mary, confess, after mature deliberation, *That the Church he had established, was erroneous and wicked: and that therefore he freely and publickly abjured her faith*; and testified it, by signing his Recantation with his own hand, at six different times, and in six different forms; and afterwards voluntarily becoming a Catholic, without any force or violence offered to his conscience. This made me to say, without any further hesitation, How can I continue in that Religion, (with a quiet mind) which the maker and former thereof said was both wicked and erroneous; and which I found to be the spurious upstart race of Lollardinism, Lutheranism, and Zuinglianism. And I was further convinced of the necessity of leaving the Church of England, when, in looking for Luther and Calvin's characters, (the two first grand Reformers) I found them to be such men, that they had more occasion to have set about reforming their own lives and manners, than to set themselves about reforming the Church of Christ: and without much trouble, I could easily discover the reason of their dissenting to be this, namely, their not chusing to conform themselves to the Church of Christ, but rather chusing to make churches that should suit with their lives, and conform to their haughty and vicious inclinations. Neither of them, I observed, ed, liked Confession, by reason that it was a troublesome and hard task; therefore they proclaimed it quite unnecessary. Fasting also seemed to these lovers of pleasure, too great a curb to their licentious appetites, and therefore they laid it aside, and left it in their Liturgy only as a piece of advice to be followed by those who thought fit.

Transubstantiation they did not like, because it was a point beyond the reach of human capacity, and therefore they would not believe it; and Calvin went so far as to reject the plain words of Christ himself, when he said, *This is my body, this is my blood*; and by a most wonderful interpretation hath made it to signify, that Christ's meaning was, *This is not my body, this is not my blood*, but only the figure and type thereof.

A farther reason for my leaving the Church of England, was, because I could not conceive how a Church, founded by Jesus Christ, or a reformation, begun by the Spirit of God, could stand in need of being supported by lies and calumnies; by false insinuations and scandalous reflections; all which I found to be put in practice by the first Reformers; not to mention the force which was used to bring people from the doctrine and religion of their ancestors, and the penal laws which were made to hinder Catholics from preaching, writing, or printing, in their own vindication.

cation. And in order to make good what I say, I shall here remark, that I had always learnt, from the books that had come into my hands, that Bishop Cranmer died a martyr for the religion of the Church of England, as also Hooper, Latimer, and Ridley; when, at the same time, it is plain, upon the face of history, that they were all four tried and executed for being traytors to their king and country: namely, for being the principal contrivers of settling the crown on Lady Jane Gray, and proclaiming her Queen, in opposition to their true and lawful Sovereign, Queen Mary. And besides this, I found that Bishop Cranmer, the grand Reformer, was so far from dying for the religion of the Church of England, that he was a Roman Catholic when he was tried, a Roman Catholic when he was condemned, and a Roman Catholic when he went to the stake to be executed. And, pray, let me ask any man, how he could be said to die a martyr for the religion of the Church of England? For if he really had died a martyr for her faith, he must have been tried and condemned for defending it; which he was so far from doing, that, before his trial came on, he recanted that very religion, and said it was both *erroneous* and *wicked*. Yet, strange to tell! he is for all this deemed a martyr by many authors, who have been employed to poison the minds of the people. And one Fox has placed him amongst his list of those which he calls martyrs for the Church of England; which list he has drawn to a great length, filling it with those who died for treason, rebellion, and the like: which proved to me, that the Reformation could not be dictated by the Spirit of God, seeing she was forced to take in so many *traytors* and *rebels*, as *witnesses* of, or *martyrs* for her doctrine; for which reason I was determined to embrace the ancient religion, *whose martyrs were quite of a different stamp.*

Another reason why I left the Church of England, was this: I found, on the face of history, that she had encouraged all manner of impiety, even from her first appearance, in order to draw men from the ancient way which their ancestors used to serve God in: For so abominable, and impiously wicked were they in the first reforming age in this land, that Guthrie observes, *That churches were converted into stables, and theatres for prize fighting; and all people seemed, at that time, to have lost sight both of morality and piety. And the system of government,* he says, *was both arbitrary and bloody; and the great men of that age followed the Court, as crows do carrion, that they might prey on the possessions of religion.* And so far were all plunged in the gulph of wickedness, that the same historian observes,

observes, *That the universal corruption of those times was beyond description and beyond example.* And he further remarks, *that it plainly appeared, that it was ambition, and not religion, that was the main view of the Reformers.* Alas then, said I, how can I dare to continue in that religion, which was set on foot through *ambition* and *avarice!* when it plainly appears that the first promoters of it were men of such vile characters, that none ever had equalled them; neither could the pen of history describe the many *wickednesses* and *impieties* which they who called themselves Reformers were guilty of: Then I cried out after the manner of holy Jacob, saying, " *Oh, my soul! come not thou into their secret; unto their assembly, mine honour, be not thou united:*" for in their craft and hypocrisy they have overwhelmed this land in *irreligion, Atheism, Deism, infidelity, and all sorts of Sectaries.*

Another reason why I left the Church of England, was, In my reading history, I discovered the many notorious falsities that I had formerly been taught to believe concerning Queen Mary, whom I had been taught to look upon as the most barbarous and bloodyest of women; and had oft heard it affirmed, that she was the most cruel creature that ever existed; when, in searching history, I found that the whole number of those who she executed during her reign, amounted to no more than 273, and 64 more whom she otherwise fined and imprisoned (according to Speed's history, who is deemed a true author). At this small number I was astonished; especially when I found, that in the second year of her reign, Wyat, with several thousand men, rebelled against her, and came even to her palace, and demanded her prisoner; but in a few hours after that bold insult, he and most of the leaders were brought prisoners before the Queen. Upon this I began to compare facts, when I soon found that Mary could not deserve the character of bloody, &c. for if she did, I perceived that Queen Elizabeth deserved it more so; for I found that she executed double the number that Queen Mary did, even on account of one rebellion, namely, that of the Earls of Westmoreland and Northumberland, which proceeded no farther than the North of England. Besides, Queen Elizabeth I find executing, in the most cruel manner, numbers of priests and seminarists, purely because they were Catholics. Now if Queen Elizabeth deserves the name of good, even after she had been guilty of the most severe persecutions; surely then, we have reason to say with Sir Richard Baker, in his Chronicles, "That Mary was amiable; and that we "must not deny her to be a merciful Prin-"cess." Neither ought we to impute the

death

death of those who died in her reign for *rebellion*, to the cruelty of the Queen, or her hatred to the *reformation*. Now after discovering the means that were used, and the artful calumnies that were raised, in order to blacken the character of this *catholic Queen*, I fairly concluded, that those who used such unjust methods, could not have truth on their side; and from hence I inferred, that these men were not of the true Church of Christ, which should continue to the end of the world, teaching, and being taught, all truth. Therefore I held it both dangerous, and unsafe, to be in their communion, because *all liars, shall have their portion in the lake of fire and brimstone*, Rev. xxi. 8.

Lastly, The chiefest of all my reasons for leaving the Church of England, was, *The many alterations that have been made in her faith*. And it was these very alterations that confirmed me in a firm belief, that her first guides and institutors, were not guided by the Holy Ghost, as they boastingly pretended; for if they had been guided by the Spirit of Truth, they most certainly would have been directed to have fixed upon a true faith, which faith no one could have presumed to alter, without being guilty of heresy. But the faith which these first reformers fixed upon, has been altered; first by themselves, *three years after it was made*, and then by by Queen Elizabeth, &c. (as see in Sparrow's Collection of Articles, &c.) Now when I had observed this, the following question naturally offered itself, namely, Which of these faiths can be right? Why, the present to be sure, I thought, must have the best title. But then upon examination I found, that if the present faith was right, then that which was before it, in consequence must be wrong, or else it would have needed no alteration. Now if the former faith which the Church of England fixed upon, was wrong, the present cannot be right, because it sprang from that which is false; and Christ himself has said, that a corrupt tree cannot bring forth good fruit; for which reason I concluded, that the present faith of that Church had no better a title to the truth than the first had, which was made in King Edward's time.

To give a proof of the alterations that have been made—Behold, in 1547, the injunctions ordained, " That the two lights shall be " upon the high altar, before the Sacrament, " for the signification, that Christ is the very " true light of the world; therefore, they " shall be suffered to remain."—*Item*, " That " they shall, in confessions, every Lent, ex- " amine every person that cometh to con- " fession to them," &c.

The same injunctions say, " Ye shall pray " for all them that be departed out of this
" world,

"world, in the faith of Christ; that they
"with us, and we with them, at the day of
"judgment, may rest both body and soul,
"with Abraham, Isaac, and Jacob, in the
"kingdom of heaven."

"*Item*, That the bread, that shall be con-
"secrated, shall be such as heretofore hath
"been accustomed; and every of the said
"consecrated breads, shall be broken into
"two pieces at the least, or more, by the
"discretion of the Minister, and so distri-
"buted. And men must not think less to
"be received in part, than in the whole;
"but in each of them the whole body of our
"Saviour Jesus Christ."

And the prayer at consecration was then in these words: "With thy Holy Spirit
"vouchsafe to bless and sanctify these thy
"gifts of bread and wine, that they may
"be unto us the body and blood of thy most
"dearly beloved Son," &c. And as these things were deemed right and good, and to be retained amongst the first Reformers, who were the primitive Protestants, why is there such an alteration now? For if the first guides were right, and aided by the Holy Ghost, *as they positively said they was*; then, most certain, the present Protestants are wrong. And again, if the first guides were wrong, then the present Protestants cannot be right, because they sprang from them, and are a

branch

branch of that same tree, which bore false fruit; delightful to the eyes of the libertines, the free-thinkers, the deist, and all the brood of fanatic enthusiasts.

Then answered I, What can I say to these things? If I am contented to trust to that faith in which I happened to be born, which makes the passage to heaven seem easy, even as riding in a *post-chariot:* and, through the prejudice of my education, think ill of Catholics, who observe the religion of their ancestors, and by penance and mortification labour hard to gain Heaven, what will be the consequence? especially as I am fully persuaded of the necessity of imitating the life of our great Master and Redeemer *Jesus Christ.* The consequence I dreaded; and then was firmly bent to lead a new life, and to do penance in this world, in order to satisfy God Almighty's justice hereafter: for after the guilt of sin is remitted by God, the punishment is not always forgiven, as in the case of Adam, David, &c. Then I cast about for a favourable excuse for my declaring myself a Catholic, being then (as most of the kingdom are) more fearful of being despised, and losing my friends, than of losing the rewards promised by God to the true believer. But at length I found great comfort in thinking of the following promises, made by Christ himself, in the 6th chap. of St. Matthew,

Matthew, and the 33d verse; where he saith, *But seek ye first the kingdom of God and his righteousness, and all these things shall be added to you.* And from this I concluded, that as my intentions were to serve God more diligently than heretofore, and that what I altered for, was purely to seek the sure path to Heaven; why then, thought I, should I doubt of God's promise, who is not only able, but sure to perform it, *because he promised it*.

Upon this, I ventured to declare my mind, upon a proper occasion, and could not think that any person of candor and sincerity would blame me for embracing the religion of my ancestors, which I was convinced was the only true Church of Christ, in order to lead a more holy and edifying life. These are the chief motives that induced me to embrace the ancient doctrine of christianity; and these *are the very reasons for which I left the Church of England*.

The reason why I did not declare myself sooner, was, the hardness of parting, on a sudden, with the prejudices of birth and education; for as I had always been a firm assertor of the Protestant principles, this made me ashamed to think of parting with her faith, although I knew it then to be false and erroneous; therefore, I was for some time fluctuating between truth and falshood,

hood, and laboured under great agitations of mind, not daring to break the ice, and declare in the behalf of that religion, which I was convinced was infallibly true: therefore, I waited for some time, to find out a favourable excuse; and as soon as I heard of Mr. S———r's promotion to the See of Canterbury, I then declared my intentions, and, for an excuse, told those, who enquired the reasons of my leaving the Church of England, that I did not choose to be amongst them, whilst they had a Dissenter for their head Bishop. And from this many have reported, that I left the Church of England from an antipathy that I had to the Archbishop of Canterbury; but I now assure the world, that I did not; and declare positively, that I made use of those expressions only for an excuse to my friends.

And now I shall conclude this first part, with a few short observations out of history, which I think sufficient to cause any one, who loves his own soul, to leave all new upstart doctrines, and cleave unto the ancient *Catholic Church of Christ*.

First, When King Henry had took upon him to be the supreme head of the church, he, by virtue of that power, caused (as Guthrie observes) *the pastors to administer balm or poison to the flock, just as he liked. And was likewise so vain, as to stile himself the most learned*

*learned Prince in Europe, when, at the very same time, he was destroying the monuments of learning, piety, and hospitality.* And the same Historian observes, *That the whole scope of Henry's designs were to satisfy his lusts: And as to religion, he had none, though* (as he says) *when he dy'd, he, like all other bankrupts to divine mercy, threw himself on the merits of our Saviour, bewailing the errors of his past life, when the ink was scarcely dry upon the warrant, for a detestable murder, that of the Duke of Norfolk.* And Smollet says, *He was rash, arrogant, prodigal, vainglorious, pedantic, and superstitious. He delighted in pomp and pageantry, the baubles of a weak mind. His passions, soothed by adulation, rejected all restraint; and as he was an utter stranger to the finer feelings of the soul, he gratified them at the expence of justice and humanity, without any remorse or compunction.* And as such, and worse, is the character of this postilion, or first leader of the reformation, sure every religious and thinking man must detest and abhor to ride in his chariot, or follow in the road which he hath traced out.

Secondly, Archbishop Cranmer, who is stiled the apostle of the reformation; his character in Guthrie is, *That he himself was as great a freethinker, in matters of religion, as any in the age in which he lived.* And Cranmer himself, before he dyed, owned, *That the church he had established, was both erroneous and wicked.* Surely now one would think, that it was impossible for men, who profess that they hope to gain heaven, to imagine they should gain it by that religion which the maker thereof abjured, because he said, he knew it to be both erroneous and wicked; or that they should hope to be saved by following a freethinker's church, before that which was established by Christ and his apostles.

And as Cranmer was a freethinker, his character further is, that he also was very obsequious, sacrificing every thing to the will of his master; disannulling as many marriages as he pleased, setting his hand to as many condemnations as Henry chused, and signing as many laws as the King wanted to have made. And all this while Bishop Burnet tells us, *he was a Lutheran in his heart.* Nevertheless, was so compleat in every compliance, that he would even set his hand to articles of faith which Lutherism utterly condemned; yea, and he approved the mass as long as his master lived, although it was an abomination to the new Reformers. He also swore obedience to the Pope, although he looked upon him as Antichrist; and he begged the intercession of saints, and incensed their images, although Lutherans deemed

that

that practice nothing less than idolatry. He also consecrated priests, giving them power to change the bread and wine into the body and blood of Jesus Christ, by their holy benediction. He likewise gave them power to offer the sacrifice of the mass, as well for the living, as the dead; and notwithstanding this hypocrisy of acting, contrary to his conscience, the same Bishop Burnet calls him *a second Athanasius, a second Cyrill, one of the most perfect prelates the Church ever had.* Though it had been much more to his purpose, if he had shewn him a man of that boldness, as to protest against every thing that was contrary to Lutherism, and that he had vindicated all which in his conscience he believed. But thus it is, though strange to tell, a man, who practises for a number of years what he believed all that time to be sacrilege, and an abomination: yet, because he commenced a new Reformer, is by them stiled a second Athanasius, &c. although, if people were not blind, they might easily discover the difference betwixt a dissembling hypocrite, and a defender of the primitive doctrine and discipline of the Catholic Church, as St. Athanasius, and St. Cyrill were: but when darkness hath overcast men's minds, the dire contagion spreads, insomuch that they embrace every absurdity.

Thirdly,

Thirdly, The character of King Edward the sixth's ministers, who ruled him, and pretended to establish the reformation in his name, is enough to fright any reasonable man, from the faith which they established. Hear what Guthrie says of these reforming gentlemen: *Nothing* (says he) *in their time was too impious to get money*; and he likewise observes, *that Northumberland, the Prince's Prime Minister, made a very gainful trade by granting licences in abundance for eating flesh in Lent. And at this time* (he says) *that nothing was wanting to encourage impiety: that the whole system of Government was both arbitrary and bloody, and that the people lost sight both of piety and morality: and every pragmatical fellow preached up whatever came in his way, so that* (as he says) *the universal corruption of those times is beyond description, and beyond example.* Strange! Oh strange to think! that any sensible man should offer to boast of the purity of that church, which is built upon *impiety, prophaneness, and immorality*. When the very men, who laid the foundation of it, were so abominably wicked, that the corruption of manners which they caused, was too great to be described by the pen of history! and too impiously wicked to find any to whom they might be compared! Alas! nothing but a miracle can convince those, who can overlook these facts.

And

And one would think, that nothing but the laws that are made to hinder Catholics from writing, printing, or speaking in their own justification, could hinder the truths of their religion from being made manifest. Smollet observes also, that King Henry's Parliament was so complaisant as to give away the liberties of the nation, in every respect. For he says, They first made the King absolute master of their lives and fortunes, and now (says he) they subjected their consciences to his will and pleasure: for he observes, they made an act, that every thing that the King should ordain on the subject of religion, should have the force of a law.

Fourthly, The observations that any one may make of the Reformers in the next age, is a sufficient proof that what they taught was absolutely false: for observe, when Queen Mary came in, the most zealous for the reformation under Edward, became now the greatest assertors of Popery; and this made people, (as Guthrie says) " look upon religion as only a scourge of " Government." And he further observes, " That it now plainly appeared, that it was " ambition, and not religion, that was the " main view of the Reformers." And he elsewhere says, " That it was no wonder " that Mary was severe, for the heads of the " Protestants in Edward's time attempted
" to

"to take from her an inoffensive liberty of worshipping; for they would not suffer her to worship God in her own way, no, not within her closet." Now as these men, who were so strenuous for the reformation under Edward, nevertheless became strong Catholics under Mary, surely, one would think, that no man need to be told that it never could be religion that these men strove to reform, for it plainly appears, from history, that they had only *ambition and avarice* for their *guides and directors:* for all which reasons, no one, that hath his eyes open, or that is willing to gain an eternity of happiness, can follow what they taught, and at the same time believe it to be the doctrine of *Jesus Christ and his Apostles,* except they are deceived by the delusions of the world, and the prejudice of their educations: and for all such I will pray, that God may convert their hearts, and open their eyes.

Fifthly, The severe laws that were made by Queen Elizabeth, and the terrible persecution that she raised against all those who practised the old religion, which all her noble ancestors had both lived and died in, is enough to shew that charity was quite a stranger to these broachers and establishers of the Protestant religion. For in 1580, Guthrie observes, *that the persecution ran*

*so*

*so high, that the Jails in the North were so full of Papists that they could scarcely hold them, so that they were obliged to admit many to bail who were in for lesser offences, such as robbery and the like; and that many were executed, and some racked.* And in the year 1593, she made a law which ordained, that all those who were above sixteen years old, should be obliged to come to church; and if they desisted one month, they were to be committed to prison without bail, or mainprize, till they did reform; if any refused, they were to abjure the Kingdom; and, if they returned, were to be deemed felons, and suffer as such. All Recusants (that is, those that dissented from the Church that Elizabeth had established) were confined within five miles of their own dwellings, on forfeiture of all their goods and chattels. And about this time she caused many Priests to be put to death, and practised more than ordinary severity against Recusants of all kinds. So you see the troubles were not only great, but also of long continuance. And the same Historian remarks, "That
" the vulgar were industriously taught
" to look upon Papists as Dæmons, and being
" possessed with such a prejudice against
" them, they seemed (he says) to enjoy with
" pleasure the daily torturing and executi-
" ons, inflicted on Priests and Seminarists;"

E And

And he further observes, "That the Government did not fail to improve this spirit of the people to very unwarrantable
lengths. And every corner was filled
with spies, and every jail with prisoners."
And the same Historian elsewhere says,
"With reluctance I am obliged to observe,
that I find some of the reforming Bishops,
for a few doubtful points of Religion,
dragging innocent people to the stake,
where they were burnt to death with (as
he terms it) all the circumstances of Popish cruelty." He also notes, "That
Queen Elizabeth, at one time, executed
sixty-six petty Constables and one Priest
in the city of Durham." If this was not
acting in a bloody manner, then I am no
judge of the thing. But after all, Queen
Elizabeth passed an act to make all the mur-
ders that she committed, appear to the vulgar in a different light; by which her fa-
vourers think to screen her from being
deemed a persecutor on the score of Religion, *for the act made it high treason for a
Priest to be in England, whether he exercised
his function or not.* For which reason, her
friends say, that those who died, were executed for treason only, and not for Religion: yea, and Lord Burleigh wrote a book
on the vindication of the Queen, in which
he endeavoured to prove, that all that died,

did

did suffer only for treason: which book Guthrie calls *a weak piece*. For if we allow that it is only seeking the life of the Prince that is to be deemed high treason, how could these men come within the compass of that act, who were not allowed the least opportunity of appearing even out of their own dwellings? All which makes it plain, that these Reformers were both *cruel, and uncharitable*, and that they were *compleat hypocrites*, whose views were only *ambition:* for which manifest reasons I think that none who have sense and can judge for themselves, can be of that religion which Queen Elizabeth established, except they are such as will not take any trouble to inform themselves of what is truth: or are those who only take in their religion as babes do their mothers milk, because they happened to be born in it; or else prefer interest here, before rewards hereafter. To sum up this point, let me ask, how can any sensible person be of that Religion which was established by *a perfect hypocrite* (as Guthrie calls Queen Elizabeth) *and one who did the blackest deed that ever stained the pen of history?* This shews that she was not of God, but that she was of him whose lusts she did not fail to fulfil, whose end was horrible to think of, being overwhelmed with *black despair, and the horrors of melancholy.*

Sixthly and Lastly, The character of the very grand reformer of all, even Luther himself, is enough to make any understanding person disbelieve the doctrine he preached: for Guthrie says, *that it was despair that made him a Reformer;* and he says, *that of all the Reformers that came to dispute with Bishop Gardener, not one of them but was overcome by him, of which number was Martyr, Bucer, &c. all whom he fairly foiled.* Now as despair was the occasion of Luther's changing his religion, and as all his most noted disciples and followers, were foiled by a single bishop of the old religion, surely, that is enough to shew any man that is not wilfully blind, that these Reformers (as they called themselves) were not sent by God, but that they were *the false prophets of the beast, which should arise after the first thousand years, who should encompass the camp of the saints about, and the beloved city; upon whom, in the end God shall rain down fire and brimstone: and they shall go to dwell with the Devil that deceived them,* Rev. xx. Surely if nothing else will draw a man off from the errors which these vile men taught, the judgments which God has pronounced against the unbelievers, will I hope fright them to their duty; for behold, *Christ the Judge will come to give unto every man according as his work shall be.* Beware, then, of all those who

who build upon a false foundation, which cannot stand without the help of slander and calumny; and follow after truth, which needs not such a support, being always able to stand alone; whilst the false religions fall from one thing to another, and dwindle into sects without end, which all preach up condemnation to one another: and every new sect will claim to be the most pure and holy of all others; *giving ear to the call of the spirit of enthusiasm, and delusion.* From which spirit, I beg that God in his own good time will deliver all the inhabitants of this land. Thus far as to the first part, what follows are my reasons why I shall always live and die a Catholic.

The first of my reasons for continuing stedfast in the Catholic Church, is this: That I find in it the greatest of all satisfactions; for so pure is her faith, so sound her doctrines, so efficacious her sacraments, and so decent and instructive her ceremonies, that whoever has but the happiness of serving God in this holy Church can never leave it, unless he is led by the same evil spirit that has deceived the nations; or sells himself to work wickedness in the sight of God; or is drawn off from the truth through interest, through pride, through presumption, or despair.

Furthermore, the unity of the Catholic doctrine, and the unanimous and universal

consent

consent of all her members, in points of faith, is to me a plain mark that she is that one Church of Christ, which I ought to prefer before all others; for in any other particular sect, out of the multitudes with which Christendom is at present infected, we shall hardly find two individual persons who agree in their doctrine, or in the Articles of Faith, which every Christian is bound to believe: besides, all these sectaries differ from one another in points of faith, and yet all pretend singly to be the only true Church of Christ upon earth; yea, and each one condemns the other's doctrine. For an instance of the truth of what I say, observe what follows:— The Church of England, here claims to be the only true Church of Christ, and says, *that both Luther and Calvin (the first grand Reformers) taught damnable and erroneous doctrines, and that they were both blasphemers.* And from hence, I think, it is plain that they never could be sent by God to reform men's manners, and guide them unto all truth; for if they had been sent by God, he would never have permitted them to preach up such erroneous doctrine; and so many detestable tenets as are every where to be seen scattered up and down in their writings. For we never read in scripture of God giving a commission to wicked *blasphemers, and erroneous* men, to propagate his religion: but on the

the contrary, that all those whom he ever did commission, were men eminent for virtue in a high degree; all which men he proved to be in his favour, by giving them the gift of working *miracles:* which gift, neither *Luther, Calvin,* nor any of their followers ever obtained: because, *we know that God doth not hear sinners,* John ix. 31. But as they could not prove their mission by any miraculous gift, they set themselves to preach against all miracles, and boldly insisted that all such ceased with the Apostles; though nothing is more certain than that the conversion of this nation by St. Austin, was attended by a number of miracles: and so have all Heathen nations in general been converted by miracles. For it would be a greater miracle to have a Heathen nation converted to Christianity without miracles, than by one. But as these impostors could not produce one divine evidence in their behalf, they strove to make up that defect, *by false assertions, and sly insinuations;* and imposed upon their hearers, by boldly insisting that God had sent them in a particular manner to open the eyes of mankind, and to conduct them a straight and easy way to Heaven: yea, and they preaching said, that they were the only men on earth that could guide men the right road to Heaven, though at the same time, Luther preached up a different

ferent doctrine to Calvin, and Calvin preached up quite different from Luther's doctrine: yea, and stranger than this; Luther preached up that Calvin and his followers were damned, and Calvin preached up that Luther and his followers were damned; which shewed it very plain, that neither of them was the true Church of Christ, and that each lacked the guidance of the good Spirit, which our Saviour said should guide his Church unto all truth, and continue with her unto the end of the world. For if they had been guided by the Holy Ghost, they would not have contradicted, and anathamized one another: for observe, wherever the Apostles preached, or wherever they wrote, still the good Spirit of God directed them to all truth, so that they all preached in *unity of faith*, and all wrote the same Gospel, though in different countries, and never did one contradict the other *in any matter of faith*, but all taught the same doctrine in all places and at all times: which is a very plain proof that the same good Spirit, which guided the Apostles, did not guide Luther and Calvin; for if it had, it would not have suffered them to have preached up two different faiths, neither would it have permitted that they should strive (as they vainly did) to make the God of all truth contradict himself, by each arrogating to himself the right of being the only man in the world who could claim the name of the true Church of Christ. Whereas, if both these men's Churches had been true, God must have contradicted himself, (which is impossible) because each of them preached up a quite different doctrine. But these men's impiety did not stop here, for each of them vainly strove to prove, that there never had been a true Visible Church upon earth since the age succeeding the Apostles; if this be true, what sense can we give to that of St. Matt. chap. v. 14, 15, *Ye are the light of the world. A city that is set on a hill cannot be hid. Neither do men light a candle, and set it under a bushel, but on a candlestick, and it giveth light to all who are in the house?* Or to that of the same Apostle, chap. xviii. 17. *Tell the Church if he neglect to bear thee; but if he neglect to hear the Church, let him be unto thee as a Heathen and a Publican?* Again, St. Paul tells us, 2 Cor. chap. iv. 3. *But if our gospel be hid, it is hid to them that are lost* And the Prophet Isaiah, chap. ii. 2. *And it shall come to pass in the last days, that the mountain of the Lord's house shall be established in the top of the mountains, and shall be exalted above the hills; and all nations shall flow unto it.* Again, our Saviour says, *Upon this rock I will build my church, and the gates of hell* (that is, error or *darkness*) *shall not prevail against it.* And, again, where he promises to *send unto*

F *her*

*her the spirit of truth, which shall remain with her unto the end of the world.* Which texts and promises of Christ, prove that he always will have a Visible Church upon earth, which shall be true and holy; because his good spirit shall always be her guide, directing her unto all truth. Now all this Luther and Calvin both contradicted, by striving, as they both did, to overthrow the visibility and perpetuity of Christ's Church, in setting up Churches of their own, which never had a being before their own times, and saying that these Churches were the only Catholic, and Apostolic Church of Christ; although, at the same time, it is plain that they both contradicted, what Christ and his Apostles taught; yea, also, and as I shewed before, flatly denied what each other taught. But after all these contradictions, these deceivers of mankind boldly preached, (and their successors still continue to preach) that each of their Churches is that one, holy, catholic and apostolic Church, which we in the Nicene Creed profess to believe in, although nothing is more plain, than that not one of them all has the least claim unto it. For when that Creed was first made, it was made by all the Churches in communion with the Church of Rome, which Church was that one, holy, catholic, and apostolic Church, which then was visible over all the known parts of the earth,

earth, and which Church was the only Church, which that Creed was made to believe in.

Now, methinks, it plainly appears to every reasonable and unprejudiced mind, that both the first Reformers grossly contradicted themselves, by offering to say, it was either of their Churches that was *one, holy, catholic, and apostolic*; for *one* signifies *unity*; and *holy*, signifies *a Church free from error*: for if a Church is not at *unity* within herself, then she is not *one*, and if she falls into errors, and teaches erroneous doctrine, she certainly cannot be said to be *holy*. Now I would ask any one, What title or claim can Luther or Calvin's followers put in for *one*, and *holy?* whereas each of their Churches has almost as many different faiths as it has members, and both agree that its impossible to be *holy*; wherefore it is plain that it can be neither of their Churches, nor any that ever sprung from them, that is that *one, holy Church*, which we in the *Nicene Creed* profess to believe in.

And as to *Catholic* and *Apostolic*, both Luther and Calvin, and all the churches that ever sprung from them, have not the least right unto that name: for the word *Catholic* is allowed by all to signify the *Universal Church of all ages, and more or less of all countries and places*. Now how can any

F 2 Church

Church claim the name of *Catholic*, that had not a being before Luther and Calvin diffented? the firft of which was in the year 1517: with what face of truth, I fay, can any Church of fo late a date have a claim to the name of *Catholic?* The name of *Proteftant* was not fo much as known till the year 1529, which fhews it was not the Univerfal Church of all ages; and as to being that of all countries, they have fo little right to the plea, that they never fo much as converted one Heathen nation to Chriftianity; and every different fect of Proteftants is, as it were, confined to fome remote part of the globe or other. And as to *Apoftolic*, that is to derive a fucceffion of Paftors and Teachers from the very Apoftles themfelves; neither Lutheranifm, Calvinifm, nor any Church that ever fprung from them, can with any reafon fo much as pretend unto. For both Luther and Calvin themfelves preached up that all Churches before their times were erroneous, (and according to their known doctrines, they muft have been fo, or elfe they would have had no occafion to be reformed) and if Luther, and Calvin had preached truth, that would have proved that their Churches were not *Apoftolic*, except God had in a miraculous manner fent fome of the Apoftles to teach and confirm them; which, as he never did, they muft derive their fucceffion, either from

that

that erroneous Church which they preached against, or from him who was erroneous from the beginning.

From hence I conclude, that either the *Nicene Creed* is wrong, or else the *Reformation* must be so: but the *Creed* shews it cannot be wrong, because it is by tradition universally received, and believed by all nations, and languages, who have any just claim to *Christianity*; so that it follows, that it must be the Reformation only that is wrong; wherefore I judge it more safe to continue in the fold of Christ, than to follow any new upstart doctrine which sprang since the year 1516; because all that sprang since then are one thousand five hundred and sixteen years too young to be called *Apostolic*.

Another great reason why I continue in the Catholic Faith is this; The alterations and waverings that all her opposers are guilty of, in opposition to the *Unity* of her faith.

The Church in which I was educated shall serve for an instance of the truth of what I say. At first when she was established, she believed the real presence to be in the Sacrament; for which reason she instituted the following prayer: " Grant us, therefore, gra-
" cious Lord, so to eat the flesh of thy dear
" Son Jesus Christ, and to drink his blood,
" that our sinful bodies may be made clean
" by his body, and our souls washed through
" his

" his moſt precious blood, and that we may
" ever more dwell in him, and he in us."
Likewiſe, ſhe ordained that the following
anſwer ſhould be made in the catechiſe,
when it is aſked, What is the thing ſignifi-
ed? Anſwer, " The body and blood of
" Chriſt, which is verily and indeed taken
" and received by the faithful in the Lord's
" Supper." All which ſhews, that ſhe formerly did believe what ſhe now denies: for
if ſhe had took the ſacrament only in a ſym-
bolical or figurative ſenſe, ſhe would never
have ordained ſo ſolemn a piece of mockery,
as that prayer muſt be, if the real preſence
had not been believed when it was firſt made.
For is it not a mockery to beg of God to grant
that they may eat and drink the fleſh and
blood of Chriſt, if at the ſame time they
firmly believe that there is no fleſh and blood
to be either eat or drank? yea, certainly, it
is a great mockery for any man to beg of
God, in a ſolemn manner, to grant that they
may eat and drink that which they believe is
not there to be either eat or drank Now if
it was right, when the Church of England
was firſt eſtabliſhed, to believe in the real
preſence in the ſacrament; then it is certainly
wrong in her to diſbelieve it now: therefore
ſhe is either wrong now, or was ſo formerly;
and if ſhe is wrong now, or was ſo formerly,
it is then plain that ſhe cannot be the Church
of

of Christ, because our Saviour promised to be with his Church *always; even to the end of the world, directing and guiding her unto all truth,* and as she is not the Church of Christ, *unto which all nations shall flow,* I hold it both dangerous and unsafe to be in her communion, and therefore hold it good to continue in the antient *Catholic Church,* because I am convinced that she *is founded upon a rock, against which the gates of hell* (that is error and darkness) *shall not prevail.*

Now, in order to undeceive some of my acquaintance, I will here set down the catholic faith concerning some points, out of the many, which I know are misrepresented unto them. And first, I will shew what is the belief of the church concerning Purgatory; next Praying to Saints; next Image Worship; and, lastly, I will explain, in a short manner, the doctrine of Transubstantiation; in all which, I will give you the belief of the whole body of Catholics throughout the world; and doubt not, but it must open the eyes of many religious well-meaning people, especially when they perceive how grossly they have been imposed on by false and scandalous misrepresentations. Yea, certainly, no one can help seeing, that that religion must be bad in itself, which makes use of such base means for its support: for if a religion is true, it needs no other help but what comes from

the

the God of truth; whilst that religion which is false, is obliged, for its own preservation, to raise scandalous and evil reports, and to enact cruel and severe laws, to kill, destroy, and banish the teachers of truth; yea, and to hinder people from seeing what is good; they are obliged to burn and destroy all good books that contain the grounds of the old religion, and fine and imprison all those who will not conform to the new faith, nor suffer any to write, print, or dispute publicly against it.

First, I shall proceed to what concerns Purgatory, which Protestants, I know, believe contrary to the word of God, and call it by the name of the Pope's Prison, and say it is an absurd doctrine, grounded neither on scripture nor reason; this, therefore, I shall prove to be a mere bugbear, and only made use of to fright people from the catholic faith, and also shew that protestants assert a falsity, for I shall make it plain, that the belief of a middle state is grounded both on *scripture, antiquity*, and *reason*. But, first, I will shew you what we believe, or mean, by Purgatory: We believe it to be a middle state of souls departed, who being not entirely purified from their sins here, by penance, and good works, are purified there, by some means appointed by God, but unknown to us, and then are received into heaven, where nothing that is defiled can enter. Now

Now you are to observe, that we believe that there are some souls, who depart this life, so pure, as to be translated immediately to heaven: and others, who die in their sins, without repentance; these descend into hell; and we believe that there is a third sort, that have neither lived so wicked as to deserve hell, nor yet so good, and perfectly pure as to be forthwith admitted to the state of bliss; but are to pass through a purging fire, where, by some means known to God, they make that full satisfaction to him for their sins, which they neglected here, and then are admitted into heaven. I will here give an instance, to make what I have said appear more plain: Suppose a man to die suddenly, who has behaved like a true christian in all respects; performing whatever the christian religion requires; this man, no doubt, goes straight to heaven: and suppose a man to die suddenly, in the action of adultery, or murder, without time for repentance; this man certainly must go to hell. But, then suppose a third man to die suddenly, with a lie of of small consequence in his mouth, or in the action of cheating his neighbour of a penny; what now is to become of this man, providing he has been a good man in every other respect? Now to heaven he cannot go, because nothing that is defiled shall enter therein: Nor to hell; for surely the justice of

God will never condemn him to so great a punishment, for so slight an offence; therefore to some intermediate state he must go, till God's justice is satisfied, which is what we call by the name of Purgatory; you may call it what you please, but this is the name that the Church has thought proper to give it. And as a proof that there is such a place, from scripture see the following texts: St. Matt. x. 12. *Whosoever speaketh against the Holy Ghost, it shall not be forgiven him, neither in this world, nor the next.* Now this implies that some sins are forgiven in the other world; else why should our Saviour say, *neither in this world, nor in the next?* Now in heaven, there is no sins there to be forgiven: and in hell there is no forgiveness; therefore a third place must be meant, which is what we call Purgatory.

St. Paul saith, in the 1 Cor. i. 15. *If any man's work shall be burnt, he shall suffer loss: But he himself shall be saved, yet so as by fire.* Now in this the Apostle teacheth that some will be punished in the other world, and pass through a fiery trial, but yet so as to be saved. The question then is, where is this fiery trial to be undergone? In heaven it cannot be, and out of hell there is no redemption: therefore it must be in a third place, which we term Purgatory, or a state of Purgation.

St. Peter

St. Peter alſo ſaith, in his firſt Epiſtle, chap. iii. 18, 19. *For Chriſt alſo hath ſuffered, the juſt for the unjuſt, that he might bring us to God, being put to death in the fleſh, but quickened by the Spirit: By which alſo he went and preached to the ſpirits in priſon.* Now where this priſon is, into which our Saviour deſcended in the ſpirit to preach, whilſt his body lay in the grave, is the queſtion. We believe it to be the priſon of the ancient Patriarchs and Prophets, who died before our Saviour's coming, and could not aſcend into heaven by the deeds of the law; but by the blood of Jeſus Chriſt, who went in ſpirit to preach unto them, and ſhew them the way to eternal glory.

In the ſecond Book of Maccabees, and the 12 chap. and 43 v. it is there called *a wholeſome and holy cogitation to pray for the dead, that they may be looſed from their ſins*; which plainly ſhews, that they in the old law believed that the dead were helped by the prayers and ſacrifices of the living; and thoſe dead could not be believed to be in hell, becauſe from thence none are releaſed, neither can they be helped; and in heaven, they ſtand in no need of help: therefore, it muſt be in ſome other place, which place we call Purgatory; you may call it by what name you pleaſe: But that there is ſuch a middle place of punishment, is plain from Holy Scripture.

Now that this doctrine is very ancient, I shall prove from St. Chryfoftom, who fays: *" 'Tis not in vain that oblations are made for the dead; 'tis the ordinance of the Holy Ghoſt, who defigns we ſhould help one another."* St. Auguſtine alſo ſays, *" Oblations, prayers, and alms in abundance are the true comfort we can procure to thoſe who are dead."* And Calvin himſelf owns, in his L. 3. Infti. c. 5. ſect. 10. *that it was a received cuſtom in the Church to pray for the dead, above thirteen hundred years before his time:* which is a ſtrong proof of the antiquity of it, yea, and that out of the mouth of one of the greateſt adverſaries of the Church. To confirm what has been already ſaid, I ſhall here add another proof from St. Auguſtine, who lived in the end of the fourth century, and beginning of the fifth: and it cannot be doubted, but that he muſt have known the doctrine of the Church in his days, and yet he ſpeaks in ſuch a manner of this article of prayer for the dead, that no man in his wits can deny it to have been the practice of the Church in thoſe early ages. The place I mean, is the 13 chap. of the 9th Book of his Confeſſions: he had ſpoke before of the death of his mother Monica, and his own tears on the account, " And now O Lord (ſays he) I, with a heart
" perfectly

"perfectly healed of that wound in which a
"carnal affection perhaps might seem too
"much engaged, do pour out before thee, in
"behalf of her thy servant, a far other kind of
"tears, flowing out of a troubled spirit, from
"the consideration of the perils of every soul
"dying in Adam. Although, being re-
"vived in Christ, she had lived, before her
"releasment from the flesh, in such a man-
"ner as that thy name was much praised,
"both in her faith and virtues; yet I dare
"not affirm, from the time that thou didst
"regenerate her by Baptism, that no word
"fell from her mouth contrary to thy com-
"mands: and I find it pronounced by the
"truth, thy Son, if any one shall say unto
"his brother, fool, he shall be in danger of
"hell fire; and woe be even to the laud-
"able life of men, if thou shouldst exa-
"mine it without mercy. But because thou
"makest not a strict enquiry after sin, there-
"fore we have a confident hope to find some
"place of indulgence with thee: and on the
"other side, whosoever he be that can reckon
"up his true merits unto thee; what accounts
"he unto thee but thy own gifts? Oh then,
"that men would know themselves, and he
"that glorieth would glory in the Lord. I
"therefore (O thou, my praise and my life,
"God of my heart) setting aside here her
"good deeds, for which, with much re-
"joicing

"joicing I render thee thanks, now become
"a petitioner to thee for the sins of this my
"mother: Hear thou me, I beseech thee,
"by that cure of our wounds that hung up-
"on the cross, &c. ...... And I believe,
"that thou hast already done this, which I
"beg of thee; but let these free-will offer-
"ings of my mouth, O Lord, be acceptable
"to thee, because, when the time of her dis-
"solution drew near, she had no regard to
"her body, to be sumptuously interred, or
"richly embalmed, nor desired some choice
"monument, nor was solicitous for a se-
"pulcher in her own country. None of these
"things recommended she unto us; but on-
"ly desired us to make remembrance of her
"at thy altar; at thy altar, at which, without
"any one day's intermission, she constantly
"attended, from whence she knew was dis-
"pensed the holy victim; by which was can-
"celled the hand writing which was con-
"trary to us, &c. Rest she, therefore, in
"peace, together with her husband, before
"whom, and after whom, none enjoyed
"her, and whom she dutifully served, bring-
"ing forth fruit unto thee with much pati-
"ence towards him that she might also gain
"him unto thee; and do thou inspire, O
"Lord my God, do thou inspire thy ser-
"vants my brethren, thy children my mas-
"ters, whom I serve both with my heart
"and

"and my voice, and my pen, that as many of
"them as shall read these things, may re-
"member, at thine altar, Monica thy hand-
"maid, and Patricius her husband, from
"whose bodies thou broughtest me into
"this life, after what manner I know not;
"let them remember, with a charitable de-
"votion, these my parents in this secular
"vanishing life, my brethren under thee
"our father in our Catholic Mother, my
"fellow citizens in the eternal Jerusalem
"(which place of the pilgrimage of thy peo-
"ple so much sigheth after from their de-
"parture thence, till their return thither)
"that so what my mother made her last re-
"quest to me, may be more plentifully per-
"formed to her by the prayers of many, pro-
"cured by these confessions and prayers of
"mine." Thus far St. Augustine: which I think is more than sufficient to convince any man of common sense, that the doctrine of the Roman Catholic Church at present, in regard to this article of praying for the dead, is the same with the primitive Church in St. Augustine's days.

Now that this doctrine of Purgatory has reason on its side, observe what follows. As God is just to render to every one according to his works, and to punish sin: Those who have sinned most, will be punished most; and those who have sinned less then those, will
be

be punifhed lefs; and alfo thofe who have finned leaft of all, will be punifhed leaft: for every idle word is an offence to God, and deferves punifhment from him, and will be punifhed by him hereafter, if not cancelled by repentance here. Yet reafon tells us, that fuch fmall offences do not deferve eternal punifhment in hell, becaufe if they did few or none would efcape it, by reafon that all are apt to do fomething impure, or to fpeak fomething that they fhould not ; *for even the juft man finneth*, as the fcripture faith, Prov. 24. 16. and as nothing that is impure fhall enter heaven, reafon tells that there muft be fome third place, where thofe that are guilty of fmall offences muft be purged, and purified, before they are admitted into heaven: and this place we call Purgatory, or a middle ftate of fouls : and though Purgatory is not named in fcripture, yet the thing fignified is there. As Trinity is not named in fcripture, yet the thing fignified is there. Therefore it is not for the name that we contend, but for the thing itfelf. Neverthelefs, fome object and fay, that what faults the good die guilty of, will be forgiven at the general abfolution, at the laft day. But we defire to know in what place they are to be till the general judgment happeneth ? Now in heaven they cannot be, before they are forgiven; and in hell there is no forgivenefs.

Therefore

Therefore in a third place they must be, let the name be what it will. This is the doctrine of Purgatory, and as doubtless there is such a place, we think it incumbent on us to extend our charity to those who are suffering under the hand of divine justice: by assisting them with our prayers, and alms-deeds: and if we should pray for one that does not want it, we believe that God will be pleased with this our charity, because we do it purely out of charity, *which if we lack, all our other works are dead.* For as St. Paul says, *if we have not charity, it profiteth us nothing, though we give our body to be burned, or all our goods to the poor,* 1 Cor. 13.

Secondly, I shall explain the Catholic doctrine of praying to saints. But first it will be necessary for the better understanding of this point to consider well what sort of bodies saints have when they are in heaven. In this, sacred scripture tells us, that they are pure spirits, *seeing God as he is*, (which bodily eyes cannot) *and are rendered like unto him, knowing as they are known.* Which no other beings but spiritual ones can ever attain unto. Now a spirit is of such a nature, that it requires no extention of place, but can be in the point of a needle, as well as in a large house, can pass through marble, or adamantine walls, as easily as through the air; can see to an immense distance, although it hath

H

no eyes, can hear although it has no ears, can converse although it has no tongue, and can be at one place one moment and at the most distant, the next, because nothing lets, or hinders it. Thus, the sight of spirits is obscured by the density of the air, not their hearing affected by any tremulous motion, that sound makes in the air. But the whole world is displayed to their naked view as soon as they are disengaged from that corruptible earth which cloathed them whilst hear, and those that are pure are admitted to the beatifick vision of God, were according as the blessed Apostle St. John hath said, as above, they are made like unto him.

And as the saints in heaven are admitted to such great privileges, what difficulty can it be to imagine, that as God has revealed unto his saints upon earth those things which neither their eyes, nor ears could inform them; cannot he by the same gift, or illumination, cause them when in heaven to understand and know what is done upon earth? If Elisha, whilst on earth, and incumbered with flesh, by the light of Revelation knew what was done in the King of Assyria's bedchamber; why cannot God give more extraordinary gifts to those whom he admits into his presence? And what then should hinder the Holy Virgin, and blessed Apostles and Saints, from knowing when we desire

them

them to bestow their charity upon us in praying to God for us, that we may be heard by him in all our troubles and afflictions, for the scripture says, that charity never fails us, no not in heaven, and how can charity be exercised by any saint in heaven, except it be by praying for us upon earth? For they want nothing who are admitted into the joy of angels. Therefore the prayers that they are always puting up, must be for the members of Christ's Church upon earth with whom they are in communion; and as the Church of England saith, *that to beg our fellow members prayers upon earth*, who are as wicked and bad men as ourselves, *is not idolatry, nor any part of superstition.* Then it will consequently follow, that it cannot be idolatry, nor superstition, to beg of our fellow members in heaven to intercede at the throne of grace in our behalf. For if it is idolatry, or superstition to say, blessed St. Peter, and St. Paul, pray for me; then it must be worse idolatry, and superstition to say, I beg Parson———such a one, or such a one, to pray for me. Because we are sure that St. Peter, and St. Paul are righteous men, and the prayers of such avail much. But we are not sure that the others are righteous, and they may possibly be wicked, and then the prayers of the wicked man availeth nothing. From hence it is plain that according

cording to the known practice of the Church of England, praying to Saints in the manner that Catholicks do, and always have done, is justifiable. For if the Scripture says, they (the saints) are always offering up their prayers before God, which ascends as incense before his eyes, ought not we in all humility to ask of them to pray for us unto Christ who is their mediator, and our mediator, and this we can do without infringing on the mediatorship of Jesus Christ. For although there be but one mediator of redemption betwixt God and Man, yet there are many mediators, or intercessors, because whoever pleads for, or excuses, or lessens anothers fault, is a mediator, nevertheless, we do not beg of any of the saints to be our mediators of Redemption, but only to mediate, or intercede with God in our behalf, through the mediation of Jesus Christ. We do not crave a blessing from them independent of God, we only beg that they who are high in the divine favour, would pray to their Creator, their redeemer, their sanctifier and our sanctifier. This makes it plain that we do not put our trust and confidence in them, more than in God, as Protestants falsly assert. But that by our thus petitioning them we shew their dependence upon him, as well as ours, for by asking them to pray for us, it is plain we allow that they are less than God,

and

and cannot be confided in more than him. Does not our faying Holy Mary Mother of God, pray for us finners, fhew that we do not believe the bleffed virgin to be above her fon, or that fhe can in any thing command him? Neverthelefs proteftants are taught to believe that we honour her more than Chrift, and that we beg of her to command her fon. Alas! how blind are thofe who will not fee! and how deaf are thofe who will not hear, though the voice of reafon and truth cry never fo loud!

But it is objected and faid, how are we fure that the faints hear us? to this I anfwer, *becaufe they fee God face to face*, and in that bright mirror *know as they are known:* befides, as they rejoice at the converfion of a finner, they muft know ~~as~~ that finner is converted, and by the fame means that they come at the knowledge of that interior act, (which is oft unknown for fome time to us upon earth, notwithftanding we are acquainted with him that is converted) they know our petitions. But after all, fuppofing it fhould be as Proteftants pretend, that the faints cannot hear us; yet this is no reafon that we ought not to afk their prayers, becaufe they know that it always was the cuftom of the Catholic Church, to beg the prayers of the faints in heaven, therefore their charity which never fails, will be fure by this general knowledge

to

to move them, to petition in behalf of those who ask help from them by their pious prayers.

From hence it is plain that honouring the saints in Catholick assemblies, is honouring God, the author of their sanctity and bliss, and demanding of them the partnership of their prayers, is joining ourselves to the choirs of angels, to the spirits of the perfectly just, and to the church of the first-born which are in heaven. Therefore it is both acceptable to God, and profitable to ourselves to seek the prayers and intercessions of the saints in heaven, since both their charity for us, and their credit with God is much greater now, than when they were upon earth; and in all this the Catholic faith obliges us not to mean any more when we petition the blessed virgin, or saints, than this: *O God, may I partake of the prayers of the blessed virgin Mary: O God, may I partake of the prayers of St. Peter, &c.* from all which it is plain that we are unjustly accused of being guilty of idolatry in this point, and so I leave any one to judge what is to be thought of those who are obliged to blacken others, in order to appear more white themselves. For those that are of the true church of Christ, have no need for their support, to make use of calumny, slander, nor misrepresentation.

Thirdly,

Thirdly, I shall shew what use the Catholick Church, maketh of images, and also the worship that we pay unto them, which Protestants are taught to believe is idolatry, for I am sensible that they are taught to believe that Catholicks worship stocks and stones, and put their trust in images and pictures, of Christ, the virgin Mary, and the rest, yea and that they pray to, and confide in them. All which I will shew to be as the other, a mere bugbear, and false assertion, invented on purpose to fright weak people from the Catholick Faith. For her true faith is this, that they must by no means pray to pictures, or images, because they can neither see, nor hear, nor help them; and this all children are taught in their catechise; see the abstract of the Doway Catechism upon the first commandment. The council of Trent too hath declared the intent of images. " Images (saith the said council)
" are not to be venerated for any virtue, or
" divinity, which is believed to be in them,
" as the gentiles did of old, who placed their
" hope and trust in their idols; but because
" the honour exhibited to them, is refered to
" the prototypes or persons represented by
" them." The faith therefore of the church is this; that a respect is due to holy images, and pictures, no othrewise than with regard to the persons they represent, to excite us to devotion, and to an imitation of their holy lives,

and

and deaths. They are as books to the unlearned, and have one advantage above them: for they inform the mind at one glance, of what in reading might require a whole chapter, by movingly reprefenting to them, all the myfteries of our Saviour; his nativity, death, refurrection, and afcenfion, and put them in mind of the bleffed virgin Mary, the angels and faints, which may help to keep their minds free from vain diftracting thoughts in time of prayer, hence a good conveniency, in faying their prayers with fome devout picture before them, they being no fooner diftracted, but the fight recalls their wandering thoughts to the right object, and as certainly brings good into their minds, as an immodeft picture difturbs their hearts with filthy thoughts: and becaufe we are fenfible that thefe holy pictures and images reprefent fuch objects as we honour and venerate, we cannot but upon that account love, honour, and refpect the images themfelves. As whofoever loves their wife, child, or friend, cannot but have fome love and refpect for their pictures, and whofoever loves and honours the King, will have fome honour and regard for his image; and if you ask why we keep the pictures of our wives, children, friends, or king, 'tis becaufe we defire often to think of them, and fhew that love and refpect we have for them, and we keep the pictures of
Chrift,

Chrift and his faints for the fame reafon, becaufe we defire often to think of them, to preferve their memory, exprefs fomething of that love and honour we have for them, and to have our minds poffeffed with pious and religious affections by looking on them. Neverthelefs we do not venerate any image or picture, for any virtue and divinity believed to be in them, nor for any thing that is to be petitioned of them, but becaufe the honour that is exhibited to them is referred to whom they reprefent, yea wholly fo. And pray how does the Catholick by thus doing break the fecond command? for he acknowledges no other God but one, and to him alone he gives all fovereign honour, and the refpect he fhews to the crucifix, is becaufe he thinks no one can behold a reprefentation of our Saviour dying on the crofs, without being filled with the thought of the love and refpect which we owe to the Author of our redemption and falvation: for which reafon he holds it good to bow in honour to Jefus Chrift whom it reprefents, and in him to place his hope, and not in an image, which can neither fee, hear, nor help him. This is the ufe we make of Images, which is fo far from derogating from Almighty God's honour, that we love and honour them for no other reafon but out of respect to him, and the relation they have to those that please him.

Nay, so far are we from paying any divine worship to Images, that the Church condemns all those who *pray by, or through an Image, or who think that their prayers will be better heard or more acceptable when offered in that manner.* But then some answer, and say, that although the learned Catholicks do not commit idolatry in worshipping Images, yet it is feared that the poor and unlearned sort of them do, because they cannot all be thought to know what the Council of Trent has decreed in this case.

To these I answer, that all and every Catholick, throughout the whole World, does believe as the Council of Trent has decreed, whether they know the words of the decree or not, because all Catholicks have an implicit belief in the church, that is, they all believe as the church believes, whether they examine into the matter itself or not, and that purely on her unerring authority; an explicit faith being not required, for if an explicit faith was required, then few could be Catholicks, because there is not one Priest perhaps in twenty, that can give a plain and positive account of all the Articles of Faith which the church has ordained, therefore if I believe
as

as the church believes, it is certain that I cannot be guilty of idolatry, *becaufe the church ordains no idolatrous worſhip*, but on the contrary *anathamizes all who pay any divine honour to any thing but what is God*; and that none may be able to plead ignorance in this cafe, fhe in her paternal care has thought fitting to inſtruct all her children in her catechife concerning this article, and in treating on the firſt commandment, which by proteſtants is ſtiled the ſecond, the queſtion to the child is this,

*Queſtion*. Does this commandment forbid the making of images.

Anfwer. *It forbids the making them, ſo as to adore and ſerve them: that is, it forbids making them our Gods.*

*Queſtion*. Does this commandment forbid all honour and veneration of the faints and angels.

Anfwer. *No; we are to honour them as God's ſpecial friends and ſervants, but not with the honour which belongs to God.*

*Queſtion*. And is it allowable to honour relicks, crucifixes and holy pictures?

Anfwer. *Yes; with an inferior and relative honour, as they relate to Chriſt and his ſaints; and are memorials of them.*

*Queſtion*. May we then pray to relicks, or images?

I 2 Anfwer.

Answer. *No; by no means, for they have no life, or sense to hear, or help us.* See the Doway Cat.

Now what in the name of common sense can be more plain? Which I think is a sufficient proof that Roman Catholicks cannot be called idolaters. And altho' some malevolent lecturers of this age, who misrepresent each article of our faith, and after drawing their consequences from it, thus misrepresented, have the assurance to pronounce us worse than infidels; yet to the unprejudiced reader, these men's objections can be of no weight, because they are grounded upon what is false. *One of these once asserted in my hearing that papists were guilty of idolatry, because they prayed to images, and asked favours of them:* and if they had done so, he might very justly have called them *idolaters*, but as they abhor all such practices, and anathemise those who are guilty of them, nothing but ignorance can excuse *that person* from being guilty of slander, and defamation. As to verbal contests which oft happen, about the word worship, those persons who are so vastly squeamish, would employ their time to better purposes if they'd make a candid search after truth, and suffer it to prevail over that spirit of wrangling, and contention, which they too much encourage, for as Mr. Thorndike justly observes, " *that the words ado-*
" *ration*

"ration, worſhip, honour, reſpect, or how-
"ever you tranſlate the Latin word cultus,
"are, or may be equivocal in ſpite of our
"hearts, implying, indifferently, one kind of
"honour, to God, another to creatures; and
"the cauſe of this equivocation, the want of
"words, vulgar uſe not having provided
"words proper to ſignify conceptions, which
"come not from common ſenſes" Thorn.
Epil. p 3. And again he ſays, "That to
"diſpute whether we are bound to honour the
"ſaints, or not, were to diſpute whether we
"are Chriſtians; and wheither this be religi-
"ous, or civil, nothing but the equivocation
"of words makes diſputable; and the cauſe of
"that equivocation, the want of words."
Now there is a divine, or ſupream honour, and there is a religious, or inferior, and alſo a civil honour, and worſhip, and the honour, or worſhip which we give to the ſaints themſelves, is barely religious, and of an inferior nature, how then can any one ſuppoſe that we honour, or worſhip their relicks, pictures, or images, with any part of divine worſhip, eſpecially when he has heard that we deny and abjure any honour abſolutely due to them in themſelves, and therefore the charge of *idolatry*, or *ſuperſtition*, is *unjuſt*, *falſe*, and *ſcandalous*. Nevertheleſs ſome will ſay that we run to exceſs in the worſhip, or honour, which we pay to pious repre-
                                  ſentations,

sentations, by kneeling down to, and praying before them: but this is as the former, *a ridiculous charge*; for dumb actions are certainly undetermined in themselves to any meaning, and are only directed to it by the inward intention: as for example; we kneel down to our parents, as well as to Almighty God: and we beg the blessing of one, and the other: the material act is the same in both cases; but no one will be so absurd as to say that our petition is specifically the same, or, that our kneeling to our parent is an act of adoration, like that to Almighty God. Thus you see that words as well as actions may be understood more ways than one, and are equally liable as I observed before, to an equivocal acceptation, and although on Good Friday, just before we go to kiss the cross, we say come let us adore, we do not mean, come let us adore the cross, but only, come let us adore Christ who was crucified, and then we kiss the cross in honour and veneration of him who died upon it. But still the *Sceptic* says, that it is plain that papists worship the cross of Christ as they do Christ himself, and honour his images as God himself is honoured. But this is of the same stamp as the former, weak and ridiculous, for, by the cross, or image of Christ, the soul is only excited to pay a relative honour which terminates in God as the proper object of adoration,

ration, which is very different from honouring the images as Christ, or worshipping the cross as God is worshipped. To make this more plain, to all my readers, I will give an example, or two: A husband loves not only his wife, but also her picture; a subject respects and honours the presence chamber, and chair of state, because he respects and honours his King: so the love, respect, and honour which we have for Christ, makes us respect, and honour his pictures as representing him to us, and the cross, as the memorials of his sufferings. Now whether divines say, it is the same love which a man has for his wife, as for her picture: or whether they say it is the same honour as a subject gives to the chair of state, as to his king: or whether the honour a christian has for God, and his Redeemer, be the same that he has for his images and cross? What matter is it to us I say, whether divines determine this respect, and honour in all these cases, to be different, or the same; since however they may term it to be the very same; yet in fact it is very plain, a husband loves not the picture *as he loves his wife,* but only *as his wife's picture;* so likewise a subject *honours not the chair of state as his King,* but *as something belonging to him;* so in like manner a christian *honours not a picture, or cross, as Christ, or God,* but only *as a memorial of him,* in which

consideration

consideration this worship cannot possibly have any more of *idolatry in it*, than the two former have of *adultery, or treason*. Therefore this is a plain conclusion; *As I love my wife, my love extends to her picture, and the honour I have for my King extends itself to his chair of state; so because I honour and love God*, this makes me love all those things *belonging to him*, as his *house, altar, picture, cross, &c.* and as the commandment forbids falling down to idols, or images, worshipping, and adoring them, or any creatures instead of God, we humbly obey it, *and detest, and abhor all such practices*. Honouring, adoring, and worshipping the creator of heaven and earth alone, as our sovereign Lord and God, having his pictures in honour as far as they belong to him, and are beneficial to us in his service: and here I beg leave to ask whether there is not a great distinction betwixt divine worship, and inferior worship? and whether all worship but divine worship is forbid, or not? For if all worship but divine worship is forbid, then no protestant, would promise to worship his wife, saying, *with my body I thee worship*; and if there is no difference betwixt divine, and inferior worship, he never would bow to the name Jesus, which is only a sound of pronunciation, the same to the ear as an image is to the eye. Therefore if a protestant does not commit
                                                                idolatry

idolatry by the aforesaid practices, **but only gives all lawful and due honour, to the holy name of Jesus, and worships his wife with no divine worship, but that which is due to her**, then certainly a Roman Catholic may be allowed to give all due honour to a crucifix, and worship an holy image, with that worship which is lawful, and the council of Trent commands us to give only a lawful and due honour to such holy things; therefore it is plain that, that person who says it commands us to commit idolatry, is no better than wicked slanderer: because, if it is lawful for a protestant to bow when he hears the word Jesus pronounced, then it cannot be unlawful for a catholic to bow when he sees the representation of Jesus hanging on the cross, for one is the same to the ear as the other is to the eye, for which reason that which may lawfully be given to the one, cannot be unlawful to be given to the other.

Now there is one thing behind which I have not yet touched upon, and that is this; Catholicks in general are allowed to be people of understanding, equal with the common sort of protestants at least, and certainly are capable of judging as well as they, therefore must know that the images of gold, silver, brass, wood, or stone are all senseless beings, which have no divinity in them, and which can neither hear, smell, taste, nor underſtand, and by thus judging muſt know that they cannot have any power to help or aſſiſt them, and ſo can be in no more danger than Proteſtants of aſking favours from them, putting their truſt in them, or praying to them. But as if this was not enough, to end all diſputes on this head, the Church in order to prevent any of her members from being guilty of ſo heinous a crime, has pronounced a curſe againſt all thoſe who pay any Divine worſhip to any thing but God, and notwithſtanding this evident truth, that no Catholic can be an Idolater, yet the malice of the Devil is ſuch, that he tempts or encourages many of his *Agents* to propagate the moſt bare-faced ſlanders that Hell can invent againſt thoſe who have the ſtrongeſt ties to keep them from Idolatry, and who abhor it as much as any people living upon earth: For we have not only the command of God againſt it, and the ſame aſſiſtance of our ſenſes as others, but we alſo are excluded from all hopes of ever gaining Heaven, by lying under the Anathema of our own Church, if we are guilty of Idolatry; therefore I ſay unto all, beware of thoſe falſe teachers who ſeek to impoſe upon you by their ſheep's cloathing, leſt they beguile you of your faith, and lead you into everlaſting woe and horror; and as God is merciful

and

and wills not the death of a sinner, be ye rather imitators of the holy Apostles, Saints, and Martyrs, making the science of Salvation your greatest study, bidding adieu to idle subtilties, and barren speculations.

Now from henceforward I beg of all whom this may find, that they do not take upon them to believe Catholics guilty, because wicked slanderers say so: But that they examine diligently whether those things that are advanced be so or not; and not take it for granted, because they are boldly insisted upon by every fanatic enthusiast. And if you will but judge impartially, I doubt not but that the Catholic religion will appear to be free from every hellish doctrine, and practice; and then with very little trouble, you may see the many vile artifices that have been used to draw men off from the old religion. And I hope that every sensible man will have sense and courage enough to embrace that faith which was delivered by the Apostles, and handed down to us through an uninterrupted succession of Bishops, Priests, and Deacons, which faith is pure, holy, universal, and the only one which has the mark of Christ's true Church upon earth, that is, to be at unity amongst its members in point of faith.

Fourthly, I

Fourthly, I shall now explain the doctrine of Transubstantiation, and shall shew plainly that it is not repugnant to scripture and reason, and that it doth not contradict any of our senses, as Protestants vainly imagine it does. But in order thereunto it will be necessary to begin with shewing what we mean by Transubstantiation.

And first, we believe that in the sacrament of the holy Eucharist is contained truly, really, verily, and indeed, the body and blood, soul and divinity of Christ, even the very same body which was crucified on the cross, the very same body which is now in Heaven, at the right hand of the Father. Moreover we believe that by the words spoken by the mouth of the Priest at Mass, that the bread in a moment is changed and transubstantiated into the body of Christ, and the wine into his precious blood; and that under either species, a true, solid, living, and animated body, joined always to the divinity is contained.

And in this you Protestants are taught to believe that our senses are imposed upon, when at the same time it is you yourselves that are so; for I know that through a false persuasion your minds are so prepossessed, that you vainly imagine, that when we see the Sacrament, that we believe that the outward form, that is, the surface and the

qua-

qualities which we see, touch, or taste: I say that you foolishly imagine that we believe these outward qualities to be the true body and blood of Christ; nay, many of you think, that we believe them to be such flesh and blood that a corruptible man carrieth about him whilst on earth; and if this were so (as you imagine) then indeed you might have reason to cry out and say, that our senses were contradicted.

But if you will but divest yourselves of the prejudice of your education, and keep these bugbears off; and reflect that all this outward form, the surface, and the qualities which we see, feel, or taste, is really in all respects, allowed by us to be the same as they are represented to our senses, and that no Catholic believes them to be the true body and blood of Christ, but only the veil which shrouds it, or hides it from our senses; and that when we fall down, worship, and adore our Saviour Jesus Christ, whom we firmly believe to be really and substantially present by a miracle imperceptable to all our senses, we do not adore nor worship the veil which shrouds or hides it from our eyes, we only adore the God of our salvation, who in the mystery of the incarnation, hid his divinity in flesh; and in the mystery of transubstantiation, hides his flesh and blood under the forms, or appearances of bread and wine; and our faith obliges us only to believe, that under these outward forms, the body and blood of Chrift are hid, and concealed from our fenses.

Now I fay, if you would but reflect ferioufly on this our faith, you might eafily fee that Tranfubftantiation is not contrary to fenfe, for none of our fenfes are contradicted by it: Our fenfes only perceive the outward appearances of objects, and our underftanding only can judge of the inward fubftance; for the naked fubftance of any body cannot be perceived by any fenfe, becaufe if neither hath dimenfion, figure, or colour, nor any of thofe modifications which affect our fenfes, and this the great Philofopher fays, when in treating of bodies he diftinguifhes in them thefe two things, *firſt the accidents, ſuch as quantity, colour, ſmell, taſte, and ſuch like, which are the objects of our ſenſes. Second, the ſubſtance, which is cloathed (as it were) with the viſible and ſenſible accidents, but is itſelf inviſible, and the object of our underſtanding and not of our ſenſes.*

Now I muft needs own, that if, when we received the bleffed Sacrament, we fee it white, and yet believed it black; if we feel it rough, and yet believed it fmooth; if we tafted it fweet, and yet believed it bitter; I muft own, I fay then, no man could

could deny but that our faith taught us things evidently contrary to what our senses tell us: but when as you see before how the case stands with us in this article, nothing but invincible ignorance can possibly excuse those who charge us with the ridiculous absurdity of contradicting our senses, when at the same time we believe all that our senses represent unto us. Observe this also, that we do not apprehend Christ's body to be in the Sacrament after that gross, carnal, and corporeal manner as when he was living upon earth (as you vainly think we do) but in his incorruptible, immortal, and spiritual being: therefore our belief of Transubstantiation does not contradict the senses, by reason of the senses not being proper judges of things above or beyond their reach, for how can a sensible being judge of things insensible? Therefore it is only that strange chymerical Transubstantiation that you have been so oft told of that is contradictory to sense, which is what no Catholic ever so much as thought of believing; *for our faith is that we believe that Transubstantiation is not a sensible change*, that is, *that nothing that is sensible in either the bread or wine is changed*; from whence it is plain that our senses are not contradicted.

But

But perhaps you will say, that after confecration we fee the fubftance of bread, and yet believe the fubftance is not there, and is not this contradicting the fenfes? And I grant that after confecration we fee the fubftance as plain as we did before, but it is abfolutely falfe that any man ever faw the fubftance of bread either before or after confecration, for, as I faid before, he can fee no more than the outward accidents, or appearances of bread, and this we allow remains the fame after confecration as before, fo that the fenfes are not at all deceived. But if we believed that Tranfubftantiation was a fenfible change, that is to fay, a change of any thing that is fenfible in the bread and wine, then indeed our fenfes might eafily give evidence againft our faith, for they might declare that nothing fenfible is changed, but that all things fenfible remain the fame as formerly they were. But if, as I faid, our belief of Tranfubftantiation is, *that it is not a fenfible change*, then it is certain that our fenfes are not contradicted.

Therefore, all the objections and arguments, from evidence of fenfe, which Proteftants urge; are not againft our belief of Tranfubftantiation, but only againft an imaginary Tranfubftantiation of their own invention, which has no other being but in the minds of those who are in *darkness and error*.

Now to make it appear somewhat more plain on this point, you are to observe, that in the article of Transubstantiation, our understanding is the chief of all by which we judge of this stupendous mystery; and in this it is directed by a revelation from God himself, handed down to us by his Church, upon the conviction of which we determine ourselves by our own free will, under the influence of divine grace, and accept as a real truth the following assertions: That in the Eucharist *what appears to be bread is not bread, and what appears to be wine is not wine; but that the substance of the bread and wine is changed into the substance of the body and blood of Christ, who is there present in his divine and human nature, and not in figure only as Hereticks teach.* For if Christ himself has expressly declared by revelation, that his flesh is meat indeed, and his blood drink indeed, and that he would give his flesh for the life of the world, and that except we eat his flesh, and drink his blood, we have no life in us; and if when at his last supper he gave his Apostles commission to take the holy Eucharist in remembrance of him, and to do as he had done, saying, do this in remembrance of me, then certainly no man can deny these things unless God had given an express declaration

claration to the contrary; and as he never did so, it is our duty to give an unfeigned assent to all he has revealed.

Furthermore observe, that it is also very reasonable that we should depend upon Revelation before all things else; for if others had not done so how greatly would they have been deceived, as shall appear from the following instances:

First, When an Angel appeared unto Joshua, he took him by his senses to be a man, but when he told him that he was not so, but a Captain of the Heavenly Host, he fell on his face to the earth and worshipped him, and believed his hearing before his eyes.

Those who saw the blessed Virgin Mary, and knew that she had a husband and son, must suppose, if they judged according to outward appearance, that she became a mother like unto other women, but revelation tells she did not.

Again, All those who saw Jesus Christ, if they followed the dictates of their own judgments, must suppose him to be the son of a mortal father, a mere creature; all which shews that we must not always follow our senses, nor take them for infallible guides, where an exception is justly made against them from a well grounded faith, or from reason and experience.

Now it is plain that most Protestants do
in

in their faith believe some things which are above reason; for they allow that a belief in the blessed Trinity and the Incarnation is necessary, and yet in each of these mysteries they must submit their own judgments in obedience to faith, and this they do because, as they very justly say, they are well grounded upon scripture; and pray why will not they allow us to act in the same manner with regard to the mystery of Transubstantiation, which is as fairly proved from scripture as the other?

Now I know that Protestants allow God's Omnipotence, that is, they allow that God has the power of doing all things irresistibly; and let me ask then, What can resist or check God from doing that with a body which is above the nature of a body to do? And what can hinder the Almighty from doing some wonderful things with the body of Christ, which body is always united to the Divinity? May not he by his power cause it to be in many places at once, to be visible at the right hand of his Father in Heaven, and to be invisible upon our altars at the same time? And may it not be highly reasonable in Catholics to believe what the scripture teaches, so that we may form our judgments agreeable to the unerring word of God? Therefore let no one think it unreasonable for us to say, that our senses are not always to be trusted, for be it known unto you, that our faith is not to be directed by what we see, but by what we hear from God; because our senses may deceive us, but God cannot deceive.

But perhaps after all, some will say, how does this thing come to pass, or how is this change made? To this I answer, That it is not man, but God who works this divine change by man; for the words pronounced by the Priest in the consecration of the bread and wine, are taken from the sacred mouth of Christ, spoke in his name, and by his order and authority, who commanded his Apostles to *do as he had done in remembrance of him*. Hence it appears that none but a Priest can be the minister of this sacrament, who by a lawful ordination is a successor of the Apostles in the Priesthood, for they alone were present at the institution of it, and all other Ministers must have authority and power from them to do as our Saviour did, that is, to consecrate and deliver it to the people, as he did to his Disciples.

How deplorable then must that Church be which wants this divine ordination, and which substitutes in its place a feigned one, founded only on a fallen Priest, who had it not in his power to give that to others, which he was not in possession of himself, *for how can they preach unless they be sent.*

Happy

Happy then are those Christians who adore the wisdom and goodness of God, and praise his mercy and love for making himself the miraculous food of their souls; who presume not to dive into this, or any other divine mystery of their faith, infinitely beyond the reach of their comprehensions: but with an humble heart, and a sincere mind, submit their sense, their reason, and their understanding to the almighty power of God in obedience to faith; for the same omnipotent God, who said at the creation, *Let it be made*, now says to you, *This is my body*. And since he has declared his body to be meat indeed, and *that he who eateth it shall live for ever*, who will dare to say that he is not present in the adorable Sacrament on the altar?

And thrice happy are those who call to mind one of the great wonders which God wrought in the old law, in favour of his people, namely, *How he fed them with Manna for forty years in the desart*, for this Manna was a figure of this adorable Sacrament, *which is the bread that descended from Heaven to feed Christian souls to the end of the world*. The Israelites eat Manna and died, *but he that eateth this bread shall live for ever*. As the Israelites not only admired, but submitted without diving into the divine secret, which was so

hidden

hidden that they gave it the name of *Manna* (that is, *What is it?*) so we not only admire, but adore, and submit without vain search, into this *Heavenly Manna* so incomprehensible to us, because we know as the first was truly a *hidden secret* which had the taste of all meats, and yet was none of them of which it had the taste; so ours is a *hidden mystery*, which has the colour, taste, and other accidents of bread and wine, and yet faith which supplies the defect of our senses, assures us it is neither one nor the other; so here you have the doctrine of Transubstantiation delivered to you in a short manner, but whoever requires a fuller explanation I refer him to T. G. H. on the Seven Sacraments, where he may be better convinced of the truth of what I say (if he is not above conviction) and so I shall not trouble the reader a great deal further on this head, only I beg that he will pay a strict attention to the following observations:

The first is from these words, spoken by our Saviour, in the 64th verse of the sixth chapter of St. John, where he says, *The words that I have spoken to you, are spirit and life*. Now at this text I know most Protestants boggle, and say that this is a full explanation that we are only to receive the Sacrament spiritually, and not by the

mouth

mouth. But mark well what follows, namely, the Churches explanation of those words, *spirit and life, by propoſing to you a Heavenly Sacrament in which you ſhall receive in a wonderful manner, ſpirit, grace, and life, in its very fountain.* Mark well, I ſay, which is the neareſt the ſenſe of the words, this explanation, or yours, which explains away all that our Saviour had been ſaying before.

The ſecond obſervation is from Saint Paul's Epiſtle to the Corinthians, where he confirms the doctrine of Tranſubſtantiation, when in upbraiding the Corinthians he ſays, *you eat and drink to yourſelves your own damnation, not diſcerning the Lord's body*; in which he plainly intimates, that the Lord's body was in the Sacrament, otherwiſe how could they be ſaid to damn themſelves for their want of diſcerning it? for no man can be accuſed for want of diſcerning, if there was nothing to be diſcerned. Beſides, if the Sacrament was only mere bread and wine, how then ſhould a man be ſaid *to eat and drink damnation to himſelf, not diſcerning the Lord's body?* Or in plainer terms, how ſhould a man be ſaid to damn himſelf for not diſcerning what no man believed there to be diſcerned? But as the Apoſtle told them, that it was for this want of diſcerning that many of them were puniſhed with

weak-

weakness, and sickness, and death, let every man tremble to think of disbelieving what Christ and his Apostles have so plainly taught.

Thirdly observe, That in the institution of the blessed and holy Eucharist, our Saviour did not say that it was a mystical eating of which faith would make them partakers, but he emphatically said, *Take ye and eat, this is my body*, which they eat by the mouth, and not in a mystical way by faith only, although it is true that faith ought to intervene, in order to make the receiving the body of our Lord profitable to our souls, yet whether we have faith or not, the words of Christ have their effect. And if the unworthy receive *without discerning the Lord's body, they will render themselves guilty of his body and blood*, 1 Cor. xii. 24, 28, 29. Of his true body and blood, and not of a figurative one; that is, they will be guilty of affronting the person of Christ, and not his gifts.

Fourthly observe, That if the Bread remains bread after confecration, then it can no more be the body of our Lord, than the wand remaining a wand could be a serpent, or water remaining water could be blood in Egypt, or wine at the marriage of Cana; and therefore if the bread remains bread, it can be nothing else. For Christ did not

not say, in here is my body, or this contains my body, but indefinitely, *This is my body*. And although it is called bread even after confecration, this is done by the rule of appearances only, in the fame manner as the wand in Exodus, although become a ferpent, *is called wand*, and the water become blood, is called water; in the fame manner Angels in fcripture who appeared under human fhape *are called Angels*, becaufe they are fo, *and alfo are called men*, becaufe they appeared fo; fo the Eucharift *is called the body* becaufe it is fo, *and bread* becaufe it appears fo. Therefore, when we name it, with relation to what it was, and what it appears, *we call it bread and wine*, but when we name it what it is in itfelf, *then we call it the body and blood*, becaufe it cannot but be what the all-powerful words of Chrift made it.

Fifthly obferve, That the firft Reformers excluded all metaphorical eating and drinking, and afferted plainly, that the true body, and true blood of our Lord are given us to eat and drink truly for the food of our fouls; fee the confeflion of Bucer, &c. And Calvin himfelf fays, "We do
" not pretend that a fymbolical body is
" received, as it was not a fymbolical Spi-
" rit which appeared in the baptifm of our
" Lord: The Holy Ghoft was then truly
" and

" and substantially present, but he rendered
" himself present by a visible symbol, and
" was seen in the baptism of Jesus Christ,
" because he truly appeared under the sym-
" bol and external form of the Dove."
And what more can be said or desired for
a proof of a real presence? and yet he does
not admit any other presence in the supper
*than by faith,* nor of any faith in the supper *but what is in baptism.*

But the everlasting and inevitable confusion of those who defend the figurative
sense, is, the necessity of allowing something particular to the Eucharist with regard to the presence of the body; and the
impossibility of doing this, according to the
doctrine which they teach, will always involve them in endless perplexities. For instance, when Calvin says on one side, *that
the proper substance of the body and blood of
our Lord is received;* and on the other, *that
they are only received by their virtue as the
sun is received by its rays.* This is plainly
confounding himself, and uttering contradictions, because none can be so ignorant
as to imagine that when they receive the
virtue of the sun's rays, that they receive
the proper substance and whole body of the
sun. Thus it is that error always contradicts itself: for if faith makes present the
things promised, by this means judgment

and

and the general resurrection, the glory of the blessed, as well as the fire of the damned, will be equally present to us with the body of Jesus Christ, in the holy Eucharist: and besides, if this presence by faith makes us receive the substance of things, what then can hinder the happy souls that are in Heaven, from receiving, before the general resurrection, the proper substance of their bodies, as truly as we are here made to receive by faith, the proper substance of the body of Jesus Christ? For if faith renders things truly present, so as to possess the substance *verily and indeed,* as the Church of England's catechise expresses, what then can hinder the faithful from embracing any substance, or even the beatific vision itself? But after all, it is certain and plain, that although faith be never so strong and inspired by the Holy Ghost, yet it can no more unite itself to the substance of a thing, than our other thoughts or affections of the mind can. And from hence Catholics believe, that the presence of the body of Jesus Christ in the Eucharist, depends entirely on the word and promise of him who gave it. But they who support a figurative sense, make it depend on their faith who receive it. Now if the promise and word of God is not more efficacious in making the thing promised present, than faith,

I submit. But if the promise and word of God may be depended on, before that which any man can believe, then the figurative reformers must stand corrected: for if the body of Christ be present in the Eucharist in a figurative sense only, then the supper of our Lord hath nothing peculiar, and Christ is no more there than in any other actions of a Christian; and then it will follow, that it was in vain that Jesus Christ said in the supper only, with so much energy, *This is my body*; since with these all powerful words he was able to work nothing in it that is singular, so that those which are worthy will receive nothing *but bread and wine*, and those that are unworthy will not be guilty of the *body and blood*, it being impossible they should be guilty of what is not there. Zuinglius and his disciples say, *That a faithful and religious soul eats his true body sacramentally, that is, in sign, and spiritually, that is, by the contemplation of faith, which represents to us Jesus Christ suffering, and shews he is wholly ours.* And if it was so as these teach, nevertheless a faithful receiver would take no more substance, than the eye takes the substance of the sun. For if the body of Christ be only in Heaven, as they positively assert, and not in the Eucharist, but by the contemplation of faith; then it is nothing else but an imaginary

ginary presence. But Catholics believe that when Jesus Christ pronounced, *this is my body, this is my blood*, he did not design the figure of it, *but the substance*; knowing that it is as easy for him to change the bread into his body, as to change *water into wine, and create light out of nothing*. Therefore we believe the body to be present, yet in a supernatural manner, and so far spiritual; but nevertheless it is in substance, and not in an imaginary figure, for if our Saviour had never said, *this is my body*, his presence by the mind and by faith would have subsisted still just alike, and yet no mortal man could have dreamt of calling this *substantial*; but as he said, so we believe, well knowing that God cannot lye, neither can he who made the world out of nothing, want power to make one substance out of another. For O ye, whose hearts are harder than the heart of Pharaoh! dare any one of you presume to shew me how the God of all power, who by his word made all things, could want power to make that his body and blood, which he by his own express words said was such? and if he could not want power, your wickedness then is past all excuse, for by your affirming that what Christ gave to his Apostles was not what he said it was, you strive to make him a liar like unto yourselves.—

Tremble,

Tremble, therefore, at the thoughts of what ye have been hitherto guilty of! and by an immediate acknowledgment of your crimes, approach with humble confeſſion to the true Church of Chriſt, and be not obſtinate to your own deſtruction, but believe aright unto ſalvation.

'Tis true, the manner of ſpeaking which our Saviour uſed in the 52d verſe of the ſixth chapter of St. John, ſtartled and amazed, yea and even ſcandalized the Jews, and cauſed a ſtrife and contention amongſt them: how, ſaid they, can this man give us his fleſh to eat? But to this what does our bleſſed Redeemer anſwer, and how does he ſatisfy this their doubt, and ſettle the point he had propounded to them? Does he tell them, you muſt not take my words in the literal and real ſenſe they ſeem to expreſs, but in a figurative ſenſe, as when at other times I have told you, I am the door, I am the vine, and ſuch like allegorical expreſſions; or in a ſpiritual, or any ſuch like ſenſe and meaning? No, far from evading, or giving any ſuch gloſs to his foregoing words, he on the contrary repeats, and with the aſſeveration of verily, verily, I ſay unto you, *Except you eat the fleſh of the Son of Man, and drink his blood, you ſhall not have life in you.—For my fleſh is meat indeed; and my blood is drink indeed. He that eateth my fleſh*

*flesh and drinketh my blood, abideth in me, and I in him.* Which words, far from giving the Jews prefent to underſtand he meant thereby an allegorical or ſpiritual ſenſe, on the contrary, plainly ſhewed them, that what he ſpoke was to be taken according to the letter. Many of his diſciples upon this, as we read in the ſame chapter, ſaid, this ſaying is hard, and who can hear it. Yea, after Chriſt had affirmed that the words which he had ſpoke were ſpirit and life, many of his diſciples went back, and walked no more with him, as ſee in the 67th verſe of the ſame chapter. But who can ſuppoſe that Jeſus Chriſt, the author of truth and verity itſelf, would have permitted theſe diſciples to leave him, had he only meant that he was to be received in a ſpiritual or figurative ſenſe; it is plain, that they underſtood him according to the literal ſenſe, and if he had meant otherwiſe, he undoubtedly would have acted according to his uſual cuſtom of explaining to his diſciples his paraboli‑ cal expreſſions, and not have ſuffered them to have left him through miſtake: but far from that, as they would not believe his poſitive aſſertions of what he had ſaid, he left them to their own blindneſs and incredulity: no doubt but that his Apoſtles were ſurprized equally with the reſt, at thoſe words of admiration; yet, having ſeen

ſo

so many stupendous miracles wrought by him, they with a firm confidence in his omnipotency, waited the fulfilling of this promise, which he had revealed to them.

A common objection made by Protestants I had like to have forgot to take notice of; it is true, it scarce deserves it, only I know many of them lay a great stress upon the same, therefore I will just mention it: and that is, they say, Christ said he was the way, a door, and a vine; and as it is plain that he spoke these in a metaphorical sense, so the same is to be thought of these words, *this is my body*, &c. Alas! when people are to defend a bad cause they will catch at any thing, else nothing can be more plain, than that our Saviour himself gave a full explanation of the above parables; and 'till Protestants can shew me as full an explanation of these words, *this is my body*, &c. as I will shew them of *the way, the door, and the vine*, I will believe Christ's plain and express words, before their conjectures. Now when Christ says, in the 14th of St. John, "I am the way, the truth, and the life," he immediately points out what sort of way he is, and says, "No man cometh to the Father but by me." And when he saith in the tenth chapter, "I am the door," he immediately explains what a sort

of

of a door he was, saying, *by me if any man enter in, he shall be saved.* And in the 15th ch. when Christ says, *I am the true vine,* he immediately subjoins, *and my Father is the Husbandman. Every branch in me that beareth not fruit, he will take away: and every one that beareth fruit, he will purge it, that it may bring forth more fruit.* And, *now,* says he, *you are clean by reason of the word which I have spoken to you. Abide in me, and I in you;* and then he shews the comparison; *as the branch cannot bear fruit of itself, unless it abide in the vine, so neither can you, unless you abide in me:* and again, *I am the vine, you the branches; he that abideth in me, and I in him, the same beareth much fruit; for without me can you do nothing.* What can be fuller explained? and in the next verse, Christ shews the fatal consequence of being lopt off from a true faith in him; saying, *If any one abide not in me, he shall be cast forth as a branch, and shall wither, and they shall gather him up, and cast him into the fire, and he burneth.* Oh! how are they to be pitied who willingly lop themselves off from the true faith; for a false faith will save no one: beware, therefore, of the leaven of the Reformers, for it is hypocrisy.

For a Christian ought to be ashamed to think that Christ who came to instruct all the world, should labour to deceive it; and if Chrift Jefus did refolve to give us nothing elfe to eat and drink but bread and wine, is it probable that he would fay, *Except ye eat the flefh of the Son of Man, and drink his blood, ye have no life in you*, John vi. 53. Or is it poflible that he fhould tell the Jews, in the 55th verfe, *My flefh is meat indeed, and my blood is drink indeed*. Now, I fay, if he intended giving them nothing elfe but mere bread, and mere wine, he never could have ufed fuch expreffions as thefe; for Proteftants allow that when they read, in Luke the 24th, *that our Saviour is rifen indeed*, they muft believe, in a literal fenfe; and the fame they believe of the 4th of St. John, *this is indeed the Saviour of the world:* yet, when they read in the fame gofpel, *my flefh is meat indeed, and my blood is drink indeed*; they believe, by a moft wonderful interpretation, that Chrift meant, *my flefh is not meat indeed, nor is my blood drink indeed*; and fo when the Creator of the world faid, *this is my body, this is my blood*; they fay he meant, this is not my body, this is not my blood, but only the fign or fymbol, and yet thefe men make a wonderful noife about reading the fcriptures, when it is plain they are obliged to read them backwards, or they never could have framed a belief fo contrary to what our Saviour taught: for the unanimous confent

of

of the four Evangelists, and the subscription of St. Paul, prove undeniably the literal sense, not one of them ever mentioning, *this is only a sign of my body, a mere figure of my flesh*: therefore it is plain, that Protestants after all their high professions, do not believe the scriptures as delivered by the Holy Ghost, but that they only believe one part, and disbelieve others just as they like, so ought to be avoided; and although they make so great professions of serving God in the beauty of holiness, and with sincerity of heart; they still reject what God himself declares must save all men, viz. the Eucharistic sacrifice, so highly venerable among Catholics, and substitute in its place an empty figure like those of the old law, or a bare remembrance of Christ, which is a great discouragement to that devotion which is due towards the blessed Sacrament; because when people are taught to believe that they receive only mere bread and mere wine, in remembrance; they naturally think, that as they can remember that Christ died for them, therefore it is wholly indifferent whether they make use of the bread and wine or not; whereas Catholics believing that Christ is really present, to be received by the faithful in these divine mysteries, they are pressed by this motive to a daily attendance on his divine service,

service, and to a frequent and worthy participation of these holy things. As our Lord Jesus Christ has testified that his flesh is meat indeed, and his blood drink indeed, and that unless we eat his flesh and drink his blood we have no life in us; let us not make any doubt of this his faith and testimony. That the ancient and primitive doctors of Christ's Church believed Christ present in the blessed Sacrament may be proved from numerous authors; but I will content myself with producing only two, the first is St. Ignatius, Bishop of Antioch, and a disciple of the Apostles, who suffered martyrdom at Rome, 107. He, speaking of certain hereticks of those times, reckons it an error in them "That they do not al-
" low of the Eucharist and oblations, because
" they do not acknowledge the Eucharist
" to be the flesh of our Saviour Jesus Christ
" which suffered for our sins, and which the
" Father raised up again by his bounty."

From this it appears that in the time of the disciples of the Apostles, all orthodox Christians, believed and acknowledged the Eucharist to be the flesh of our Saviour Jesus Christ, even that same flesh which suffered for our sins, and which the Father raised up again by his bounty; and that none but hereticks denied it. See his Epistle to the Christians of Smyrna.

The other is St. Ambrose, Bishop of Milan, Anno 374, in his Book of the Mysteries, chap. 9; in treating of the blessed Sacrament, writes as follows:—' For the
' light is to be preferred to the shadow,
' the truth to the figure, the body of the
' Maker to the manna from Heaven.
' Perchance thou wilt say to me, I see a-
' nother thing; How do you affirm to me
' that I receive the body of Christ? We
' have this therefore yet to prove. How
' many examples have we here to produce?
' Let us shew, that this is not what nature
' formed, but what the blessing has conse-
' crated, and that the power of the blessing
' is greater than that of nature, because by
' the blessing even nature itself is changed.
' Moses held a rod in his hand, he cast it
' down and it became a serpent; he caught
' hold again of the serpent's tail, and it re-
' turned to the nature of a rod. Thou
' seest then, that by the grace conferred on
' the prophet, nature was twice changed of
' the serpent and of the rod. The rivers
' of Egypt run with pure water; on a sud-
' den, blood began to gush out from the
' veins of the springs: there was nothing
' in the rivers that could be drunk. A-
' gain, in consequence of the prophet's
' prayers, the blood of the rivers ceased;
' the nature of water returned, &c. Now
if

' if the blessing of a man was of so much
' force as to convert nature, what shall we
' say of the divine consecration, where the
' very words of the Lord our Saviour ope-
' rate? For this Sacrament which thou re-
' ceivest is made by the words of Christ;
' and if the words of Elias were so pow-
' erful as to draw fire from Heaven, shall
' not the words of Christ be powerful enough
' to change the kinds (species) of the ele-
' ments? Thou hast read concerning the
' works of the whole creation, that he
' spoke, and they were made; he com-
' manded, and they were created. If then
' the word of Christ could make something
' out of nothing, shall he not be thought able
' to change the things that are, into what
' they were not? For it is not a less task to
' give new natures to things, than to change
' their natures. But what need of argu-
' ments? Let us propose examples from
' himself, and assert the truth of this mys-
' tery by the example of the incarnation.
' Was it according to the course of nature
' that our Lord Jesus Christ was born of
' Mary? It is evident, that it was contrary
' to the course of nature for a virgin to bring
' forth.

' Now this body which we make (in the
' Eucharist) is that (which was born) of
' the virgin. Why dost thou seek for the
' order

'order of nature in the body of Chrift,
'when our Lord Jefus himfelf, contrary
'to nature, was born of a virgin? Doubt-
'lefs, it was the true flefh of Chrift that
'was crucified, that was buried. It is then
'truly the Sacrament of his flefh. Our
'Lord Jefus himfelf cries out, This is my
'body: before the bleffing of the Hea-
'venly words, it is named another kind of
'thing; after the confecration, it is figni-
'fied to be the body of Chrift. *(Corpus
'Chrifti fignificatur)* He himfelf calls it
'(that which is contained in the chalice)
'his blood: before the confecration it is
'called another thing, after the confecra-
'tion it is called blood; and thou fayeft,
'amen; that is to fay, it is true: what thy
'mouth fpeaketh, let thy inward mind
'confefs, and let thy affection feel what
'thy words exprefs.' So far St. Ambrofe.

Now as the doctrine of the real prefence was taught from the beginning of Chriftianity, I do not fee how the prefent Proteftants can reconcile their figurative fenfe with the doctrine of Antiquity, and if they cannot, then that is a certain proof that the Proteftant religion was not that which was taught by Chrift, but only a mere novelty, unknown to the whole Chriftian world, for more than fifteen hundred years after our Saviour's time; therefore

ought

ought to be avoided by all those who hope to gain Heaven, becaufe unlefs you believe what Chrift taught, without doubt you fhall perifh everlaftingly. Shall the Almighty Creator and Lord of all Nature, who produced bread out of the earth, want power to produce what he promifed, namely, to make his own body out of bread; and fhall he who made wine out of water, be unable to make his blood out of wine? certainly no, becaufe he who is the God of all power, can never want power to do what he faid he would do: therefore, what Chrift faid to his Difciples when he was giving them the confecrated bread and wine, let us believe, being affured that the God of truth cannot tell a lie; and although it be a point above your reafon, yet be not afhamed to let your reafon ftoop to your faith.

I will now proceed to difcufs fome things which I know Proteftants are taught to hold for undoubted truths. And I will begin with the reafons that they have laid down unto them why they fhould believe the Reformation here to be a good and lawful thing, and in this I think it appears, that the chief reafon that is given for it's authority, proves moft plain that it was an unlawful deed. For that which is urged in it's behalf is this, *That it was eflablifhed under*

*under a lawful Prince who was the supreme head of the church, and by all the Bishops in a Synod held for that purpose; therefore assent they say ought to be given to such a lawful assembly.*

Now you are to observe, that in this Synod or Council, there was no more than twenty-four Bishops, and two Metropolitans, which did fix upon the Articles of the Church of England; in which Articles they did presume to condemn what the whole body of Bishops throughout all Europe professed to believe; yea, and to shew their authority, obliged all their subjects to sign the said Articles under pain of the Church's censure. Now as it was deemed lawful that assent was due to this small number of Bishops, convened together by one whose spiritual authority was doubtful; sure no one will deny but that for the self same reasons, assent was also due to those hundreds of Bishops that were assembled in former Councils for weighing of arguments, &c. Especially when we consider that they were still in the same judgment, by always agreeing in the same faith. Therefore it is plain, that other Councils are rendered justified by the practice of these twenty-six Bishops, by reason that this small number required assent and obedience to their laws; for if what these twenty-six did, was binding to mens consciences, certainly then it will follow, that the Councils which were before this, were more binding; because the Bishops in some were more than twenty times the number of this, and assembled under the undoubted head of the Church, and were men also, whose consecration no one could question, which cannot be said of the English Bishops. Besides, if the laws of the land make the established religion sacred, the Catholic religion must be so, for it was established by many laws, for ages before Queen Elizabeth's time: from all which it is very plain, that the Reformation is rendered an unlawful thing, even by the very reason which is urged *for its authority*.

Next I should proceed to examine the supremacy, and whom *they* were that took upon them to dispose of that title, but as it is made *treason to write against it*, I shall content myself with presenting to you an admirable speech made in Parliament (in the year 1555, being the first of Queen Elizabeth's reign) *by the Archbishop of York, and Lord Chancellor of England*; and after the perusal will leave any one to judge, whether the spiritual authority granted to the Queen was a fitting act, or whether those who gave it her had a lawful power and right so to do.

The

The Speech begins thus:

"MY LORDS,

"With all humble submission of my whole discourse to your wisdoms, I purpose to speak to the body of this act touching the Supremacy; that so, what this honourable assembly is now adoing, concerning the passing of this act, may thereby be better weighed, and considered by your wisdoms.

"First, Then, by virtue of this act of Supremacy, we must forsake and fly from the See of Rome; it should be considered, what matter lieth therein, and what of danger, or inconvenience; or else, whether there be none at all. Secondly, If the intent of this act be to grant, or settle upon the Queen's Majesty a Supremacy, it should be considered of your wisdoms, what this Supremacy is, and whether it doth consist in spiritual government or temporal?

"If in temporal, what farther authority can this house give her, more than she already hath by right of inheritance? and not by our gift, but by the appointment of God; being our Sovereign Lord and Lady, our King and Queen, our Empress and Emperor; and if farther than this we acknowledge her to be head of the Church of England, we ought also to grant, that the Emperor, or any other Prince being Catholic, and their subjects Protestants, are to be the heads of their Church, whereby we shall do an act, as disagreeable to Protestants, as this seems to Catholics.

"If you say, the Supremacy consists in spiritual concernments, then it should be considered what the spiritual government is, and in what point it doth chiefly consist; which being first agreed upon, it should be further considered of your wisdoms, whether this house may grant it to her Highness or not, and whether her Highness be an apt person to receive the same? So by a thorough examination of these parts, your honours shall proceed in this matter groundedly, and upon such sure knowledge, as not to be deceived by ignorance.

"Now to the first point, wherein I promised to examine, what matter of weight, danger, or inconvenience might be encurred by this our forsaking, and flying from the Church of Rome; if there were no further matter therein, than the withdrawing our obedience from the Pope's person, (supposing that he had declared himself to be a very austere and severe Father to us) then the business were not of so great importance, as indeed it is, as it will immediately here appear; for by relinquishing and forsaking
the

the Church, or See of Rome, we must forsake and fly from all general councils.

"Secondly, From all canonical and ecclesiastical laws of the Church of Christ.

"Thirdly, From the judgment of all Christian Princes.

"Fourthly, and Lastly, We must forsake and fly from the holy unity of Christ's Church, and so by leaping out of Peter's ship, we hazard ourselves to be overwhelmed in the waves of schism, of sects, and divisions.—[How far the Bishop's foreknowledge was right in this point, the times we live in will declare.]

"First, Touching the general councils, I shall name unto you these four: The Nicene Council, the Constantinoplitan Council, the Ephesine, and the Chalcedon, all which are approved by all men.

"Of these same councils, St. Gregory writeth in this wise, Sicut enim sancti Evangelii quatuor libros, sic hæc quatuor concilia, Nicenum, Constantinoplitanum, Ephesinum, et Chaledonense, suscipere, ac venerari me fateor: That is to say in English, 'I confess I do receive and reverence those 'four general councils of Nice, Constanti- 'nople, &c. even as I do the four holy E- 'vangelists.'

"At the Nicene council, the first of the four, the Bishops which were there assembled,

bled, did write there epistles to Sylvester, then Bishop of Rome, that their decree then made, might be confirmed by his authority.

"At the council kept at Constantinople, all the Bishops there were obedient to Damasus, then Bishop of Rome; he as chief in the council gave sentence against the heretics, Macedonius, Sabellius, Eunomius, which Eunomius was both an Arian, and the first author of that heresy, that only faith doth justify, and here (by the way) it is much to be lamented, that we the inhabitants of this realm are much more inclined to raise up the errors and sects of ancient condemned heretics, than to follow the true approved doctrine of the most catholic and learned fathers of Christ his church

"At the Ephesine council, Nestorius, the heretic, was condemned by Celestino, the Bishop of Rome, he being chief judge there.

"At the Chalcedon council, all the Bishops there assembled, did write their humble submission unto Leo, then Bishop of Rome, wherein they did acknowledge him there to be their chief head, six hundred and thirty Bishops of them.

"Therefore to deny the See Apostolic, and its authority, were to contemn, and set at nought the authority and decrees of those noble councils.

"Secondly,

"Secondly, We must forsake and fly from all canonical and ecclesiastical laws of Christ his Church, whereunto we have already professed our obedience at the font, saying, Credo sanctum, Ecclesiam Catholicam, that is, 'I believe in the Holy Catholic Church; which article containeth, that we must receive the doctrine and sacraments of the same church, obey her laws, and live according to the same; which laws do depend wholly upon the See Apostolic, and like as it is here openly professed by the judges of the realm, that the laws agreed upon in the higher and lower houses of this honourable Parliament, be of small or none effect, before the royal assent of the King, or Prince be given thereunto; even so ecclesiastical laws made cannot bind the universal Church of Christ, without the royal assent, and confirmation of the See Apostolic.

"Thirdly, We must forsake and fly from the judgment of all other Christian Princes, whether they be Protestant or Catholic Christians, when none of them do agree with these our doings: King Henry VIIIth being the first that ever took upon him the title of Supremacy.

"And whereas it was of late, here in this house, said by a nobleman, that the title of Supremacy is of right due to a King, for that he is a King; then it would follow,

low, that Herod being a King, fhould be fupreme head of the church at Jerufalem; and Nero, the Emperor, fupreme head of the church of Chrift at Rome, they being both Infidels, and therefore no members of Chrift his church.

" And if our Saviour Chrift, at his departure from this world, fhould have left the fpiritual government of his church in the hands of Emperors and Kings, and not to have committed the fame to his Apoftles, how negligently then would he have left his church.

" It fhall appear right well, by calling to mind that the Emperor Conftantinus Magnus was the firft Chriftian Emperor, and was baptized by Sylvefter, Bifhop of Rome, about three hundred years after the afcenfion of Chrift Jefus.

" If by your propofition Conftantine, the firft Chriftian Emperor, was the firft head and fpiritual governor of Chrift his church, throughout his empire, then it followeth, that our Saviour Chrift, for the fpace of three hundred years, unto the coming of this Conftantine, left his church (which he fo dearly bought by effufion of his moft precious blood) without any head at all.

" But how untrue the faying of this nobleman was, it fhall further appear by example of Ozia, and of King David: For King

Ozia

Ozia did take the censor to do incense to the altar of God. The Priest Azarias did resist him, and expelled him out of the Temple, and said unto him, Non est officii tui, Ozia, ut adoleas Incensum Domine, sed est non est Sacerdotum & Fileorum Aaron: ad hujusmodi enim officium consecrate. That is to say, It is not thy office, Ozia, to offer incense to the altar of God. But it is the Priest's office, and the sons of Aaron; for they are consecrated, and anointed to that office.

" Now I shall most humbly demand this question; When the Priest Azarias said to the King, Non est officii tui; whether he said truth, or not? If you answer, that he spake the truth, then the King was not the Supreme head of the Church of the Jews. If you shall say, no; why did God plague the King with leprosy, and not the Priest.

" The Priest Azarias, in resisting the King, and thrusting him out of the Temple; in so doing, did the Priest play the faithful part of a subject, or no? If you answer no; why then did God spare the Priest, and not spare the King? if you answer, yea; then it is most manifest, Ozia, in that he was a King, could not be Supreme head of the Church.

" And

"And as touching the example of King David in bringing home the Ark of God from the country of the Philistines, to the city of David, what supremacy or government of God's Ark, did King David there take upon him? Did he place himself amongst the Priests? or take upon him any spiritual function unto them appertaining, did he approach near unto the Ark, or yet presume to touch the same? No doubtless. For he had seen before, Ozia stricken to death by the hand of God, for the like arrogance and presumption.

"And therefore King David did go before the Ark of God with his harp, making melody; and placed himself amongst the minstrels, and humbly did abase himself (being a King) as to dance and leap before the Ark of God; like as his other subjects did: insomuch, that his Queen Michol, King Saul's daughter, beholding and seeing this great humility of King David, did disdain thereat, whereunto King David making answer, said, Ludam, & vilior fiam plus quam factus sum, &c. That is, 'I will dance, and abase myself more than yet I have done; and abjecting myself in mine own eyes, I shall appear more glorious with those handmaids, that you talk of. I will play here before my Lord, which hath chosen me, rather than thy Father's house.

And whereas Queen Michol was therefore plagued at God's hand, with perpetual sterility and barrenness, King David received great praise for his humility.

"Now may it please your honours, to consider which of both these Kings examples, shall be most convenient for your wisdoms, to make the Queen's Majesty to follow; whether the example of proud Ozia; moving in her, by your persuasions and councils, to take upon her spiritual government; and thereby exposing her soul to be plagued at the hand of God, as King Ozia was: or else to follow the example of the good King David, which, in refusal of all spiritual government, about the Ark of God, did humble himself, as I have declared unto you.

"Whereunto our Sovereign Lady, the Queen's Highness, of her own nature being well inclined; we may assure ourselves, to have of her as humble, as virtuous, as godly a mistress to reign over us, as ever had English people here in this realm; if that her Highness be not by your flattery, and dissimulation, seduced and beguiled.

"Fourthly and lastly, we must forsake and fly from the holy unity of Christ's Church: seeing that Saint Cyprian, that holy martyr, and great clerk, doth say, that the unity of the Church of Christ doth depend upon Peter's authority, and his successors.

Therefore, by leaping out of Peter's ship, we must be overwhelmed with the waves of schisms, of sects, and divisions: because the same holy martyr, in his third Epistle to Cornelius, testifieth, that all heresies, sects, and schisms, do spring only from hence, that men will not be obedient to the Head Bishop of God.

" And how true this saying of St. Cyprian is, we may see it most apparent to all men that list to see, both by the example of the Germans, and by us, the inhabitants of this realm of England.

And by this our forsaking, and flying from the unity of the Church of Rome, this inconveniency amongst many, must consequently follow: that either we must grant the Church of Rome to be the true Church of God, or else a malignant church. If you answer that it is a true Church of God, where Jesus Christ is truly taught, and his sacraments rightly administred; how can we disburden ourselves of our forsaking, and flying from that church, which we do confess, and acknowledge to be of God, when with that church, which is of God, we ought to be one, and not to admit of any separation?

" If you answer, the Church of Rome is not of God, but a malignant church; then it will follow, that we, the inhabitants of this realm, have not yet received any benefit of Chrift, feeing we have received no gofpel, or other doctrine, nor no other facraments, but what was fent unto us from the Church of Rome.

" Firft, In King Lucius his days, at whofe humble epiftle the holy martyr Eleutherius, then Bifhop of Rome, did fend into this realm two holy Monks, Fugatius, and Damianus, by whofe doctrine and preaching, we were firft brought to the knowledge of the faith of Jefus Chrift, of his holy gofpel, and his moft holy facraments.

" Then, Secondly, Holy St. Gregory, being Bifhop of Rome, did fend into this realm, two other holy Monks, St. Auftin, called the Apoftle of England, and Miletus, to revive the very felf fame faith, that had been before planted here in this realm, in the days of King Lucius.

" Thirdly, and laft of all, Paulus Tertius, being Bifhop of Rome, did fend hither the Lord Cardinal Pole, his Grace (by birth a nobleman of this land) his Legate, to reftore us unto the fame faith which the martyr St. Eleutherius, and St. Gregory, had planted here many years before.

" If therefore the Church of Rome be not of God, but a falfe and malignant Church, then have we been deceived all this while, feeing the gofpel, the doctrine, faith, and sacraments, must be of the same nature as the Church is, from whence it and they came; and therefore in relinquishing, and forsaking that Church, the inhabitants of this realm shall be forced to seek further for another gospel of Christ, other doctrine, other faith and sacraments than we have hitherto received, which will breed such a schism, and error in faith, as was never in any Christian realm. And therefore of your wisdoms worthy of consideration, and maturely to be pondered, and be provided for, before you pass this act of Supremacy. Thus much touching the first chief point.

" Now to the Second Deliberation, wherein I promised to move your honours, to consider what this Supremacy is, what we go about by virtue of this act, to give unto the Queen, and wherein it doth consist, whether in spiritual government, or temporal : but if spiritual (as these words in the act do import, " Supreme Head of the Church of England, immediately and next unto God") then it should be considered in what points this spiritual government doth consist ? and the points being well known, it should be considered, whether this house hath authority to grant them, and her Highness's ability to receive them.

" And as concerning the points wherein spiritual government doth consist; I have, in
reading

reading the gospel, and the whole course of divinity thereupon (as to my vocation belongeth) observed these four, as chief among many others; whereof the first is, The power to loose and bind sins, when our Saviour, in ordaining Peter, to be Chief and Head Governor of his Church, said unto him, Tibi dabo claves regni cælorum, &c. that is, To thee will I give the keys of the kingdom of Heaven, &c. Now it should be considered by your wisdoms, whether you have sufficient authority to grant unto her Majesty this first point of spiritual government, and to say unto her, Tibi dabimus, &c. To thee will we give the keys of the kingdom of Heaven. If you say yea, then do we require the sight of warrant and commission, by the virtue of God's word; and if you say no, then you may be well assured, and persuade yourselves, that you have not sufficient authority to make her Highness supreme head of the Church of Christ here in this realm.

"The second point of spiritual government is gathered out of these words of our Saviour Christ, spoken to St. Peter, in the 20th chapter of St. John's gospel, pasce, & pasce, & pasce, That is, Feed my lambs, feed my lambs, feed my sheep: Now whether your honours have authority by this Court of Parliament, to say unto our Sovereign Lady, pasce, & pasce, & pasce, &c. that is to say, feed you the flock of Christ, you must shew your warrant and commission for it; and further it is evident, that her Majesty being a woman by birth and nature, is not qualified by God's word, to feed the flock of Christ, appears most plainly by St. Paul in this wise, Taceant mulieres in ecclesiio, sicut et lex decit: Let women be silent in the Church, for it is not lawful for them to speak, but to be in subjection, as the law saith; and it followeth in the same place, Turpe est enim, mulieres loqui in ecclesia, That is, For that it is not seemly for a woman to speak in the Church. And in his second epistle to Timothy, Dominari in virum, sed esse silentis, That is to say, I allow not a woman to be a teacher, or to be above her husband, but to keep herself in silence. Therefore it appears likewise, as your honours have not authority to give her Highness this second point of spiritual government, to feed the flock of Christ; so by St. Paul's doctrine, her Highness may not intermeddle herself with the same, and therefore she cannot be supreme head of the Church here in England.

"The third chief point of spiritual government, is gathered out of these words of our Saviour Christ, spoken to St. Peter in the 22d chapter of St. Luke's gospel, Ego rogavi pro te, ut non deficiet fides tua, et tu aliquando conversus, confirma fratres tuos.

That

That is, I prayed for thee, that thy faith shall not fail, and thou being converted, confirm thy brethren, and ratify them in wholesome doctrine, and administration of the sacraments, which are the holy instruments of God so instituted and ordained for our sanctification, that without them his grace is not to be received; but to preach, or to administer the sacraments, a woman may not be admitted to do, neither may she be supreme head of Christ's Church.

" The Fourth and last chief point of spiritual government, which I promised to note unto you, doth consist in the excommunication and spiritual punishment of all such, as shall approve themselves not to be the obedient children of Christ's Church: Of which authority our Saviour Christ speaks in St. Matthew's gospel, in the 18th chapter, saying, " If your brother offending will not hear your charitable admonition, whether secretly at first, or yet before one or two witnesses, then we must complain of him to the Church, and if he will not hear the Church, let him be taken as a heathen or publican."

" So the Apostle did excommunicate the notorious fornicator, that was among the Corinthians, and by the authority of his Apostleship; unto which Apostles Christ, ascending into Heaven, did leave the whole

Q                    spiritual

spiritual government of his Church, as it appeareth by those plain words of St. Paul, in his epistle to the Ephesians, chap. the 4th, saying, Ipse dedit ecclesiæ suæ, &c. He hath given to his Church, some to be Apostles, some Evangelists, some Pastors and Doctors, for consummation of the saints, to the work of the Ministry, for the edifying the body of Christ. But a woman in the degrees of the Church, is not called to be an Apostle, nor Evangelist, nor to be a Pastor, (as much as to say a Shepherd) not a Doctor or a Preacher, therefore she cannot be supreme head of Christ's Militant Church, nor yet of any part thereof. For this high government God hath appointed only to the Bishops and Pastors of his people, as St. Paul plainly witnesseth in these words, in the 20th chapter of the Acts of the Apostles, saying, Attendite vobis, et universo, gregi, &c. and thus much I have here said, right honourable, and my very good Lords, against this act of Supremacy, for the discharge of my poor conscience, and for the love, and fear, and dread that I chiefly owe to God, to my Sovereign Lord and Lady the Queen's Majesty's Highness, and to your honours all; where otherwise, without mature consideration of all these premises, your honours shall never be able to shew your faces before your enemies, in this matter, being so strange a spectacle

and

and example in Chrift's Church, as in this realm, is only to be found, and in no other Chriftian realm.

" Thus humbly befeeching your honours to take in good part, this my rude and plain fpeech, which here I have ufed, of much zeal and fervent good will, and now I fhall not trouble your honours any longer." Thus far this Speech.

And now I would afk any unprejudiced perfon, was the Supremacy, which the Lords and Commons gave unto the Queen, agreeable to God's word and the antient government of Chrift's Church? and if it was not, I afk then again, whether thofe Lords and Commons could have any other lawful authority to make the act of Supremacy binding to men's confciences? for if they had not, then it will follow, that all thofe who have been executed for fpeaking againft the faid act, have been executed wrongfully, for which fome muft anfwer at the great day of judgment. Again, as the act of Supremacy could not ftand the teft of fcripture, was not that the chief caufe why an act of Parliament was made, which denounced death againft all who fhould ever call it in queftion? And if the Supremacy is a bad thing in itfelf, I then would willingly afk, whether the aforefaid act of Parliament could make it any better in the fight of God? Or whether the ne-

ceffity

cessity of that law being made in order to support it, is not a plain proof that as it wants scripture and reason, so it supports itself by threatening death and devastation?

Hear what a Church of England Parson says on this head: "At the beginning of
" the Reformation, a new and un-heard of
" title was invented for the civil magistrates,
" and our King Henry VIIIth would be call-
" ed the supreme head in earth of the
" Church of England, and forced all per-
" sons by his acts of Parliament, under the
" severest penalties to acknowledge him to
" be so. And from this strange and before
" unknown title, which the Christian Church
" never heard of till that time, are derived
" all the pretences to spiritual power, which
" some suppose to be lodged in the King, or
" supreme magistrate, &c." As see in the Independency of the Church upon the State, page 14, wrote by Dr. Brett, and in page 20, in speaking on the supreme headship of our Kings, he says, " I am assured has no law or
" canon now in force to oblige us, and I am
" well satisfied, has neither reason, religion,
" nor gospel to induce us to use it. For if
" the King be supreme head of the Church,
" then it is impossible the Church should
" subsist without the King? for no body,
" and such the scripture tells us the Church
" is

" is, can subsist without its head. But the
" Church, we all know, did subsist during
" the time of Christ and his Apostles, and
" above 200 years after their deaths, without
" having any sovereign Prince of its com-
" munion; and consequently, without any
" headship of any temporal Prince; for
" no man can be head of a communion of
" which he is not so much as a member.
" And how a Prince can become head of
" a Church by being made a member of it,
" I cannot see. The Prince is admitted
" into the Church, just as others are, by
" baptism; but that only makes him a son
" or member of the Church: but it is
" consecration or ordination alone that
" makes fathers or heads. And therefore
" religious Princes have always esteemed
" Bishops as their spiritual fathers; and to
" this day they, as well as other members
" of the Church, call them their right
" reverend Fathers in Christ. But are
" they fathers to the *Supreme head of their*
" *Church?* This seems to be a kind of con-
" dradiction." Thus far the Doctor.

The next thing that I shall examine, is a received notion which Protestants are taught to hold for fact, " That good comes " out of evil." For which reason, they say, *That although they allow King Henry to be a most wicked, arbitrary, and lustful Prince,*

*yet*

*yet he did good, and was raised by God to overthrow Idolatry, and to free the nation from popery and slavery.* As if it was consistent with the divine Being to contradict himself. Now St. Paul expressly condemns all those who do evil that good may come: *For shall I do so,* (says he) *no, God forbid;* and Christ himself affirms, *that a corrupt tree cannot bring forth good fruit.* Now if God raised up King Henry to do as Protestants say, he must have contradicted all the other his wise ordinations, in ordaining always before then, good and pious men to preach forth his truth, and bring men out of idolatry and slavery. But this false cry of idolatry and slavery, which the Reformers here made use of, I will endeavour to obviate; for you are to observe, that King Henry, instead of freeing men from idolatry; by his example and practice established and wrought those very things which the worst of idolators were guilty of: for the character of Henry is, *that he was rash, arrogant, prodigal, vain-glorious, pedantic, and superstitious; and that he never spared woman in his lust, nor man in his anger:* and Sir Walter Raleigh says, *that if all the patterns of a merciless Prince had been lost to the world, they might have been found in this King:* thus far it is plain, that he was an

encour-

encourager of idolatrous practices, by his setting such a wicked pattern.

And Smollet observes, *That the men of this age by accustoming themselves to abject compliances, degenerated into slaves, and Henry from their prostitution acquired the most despotic authority.* (Let me ask now, where was the liberty they gained?) The same author goes on, and says of him, *That he became rapacious, arbitrary, froward, fretful, and so cruel that he seemed to delight in the blood of his subjects, and that he never betrayed the least symptoms of any tenderness in his disposition.* Now if this looks likely that Henry was raised by God to do good, and place men in freedom, then I am not capable of judging. For I rather take it that he was deceived by the Devil and his own lusts, by which he was hurried on to commit sin upon sin, until the measure of his iniquity was full, whose end was miserable, and in the next generation his name and posterity was blotted out from off the face of the earth, so that all that remains unto him, *is an infamous character, and a woful futurity.*

It is also to be noted, that all Protestants are industriously taught to believe *that Queen Elizabeth was the best of women*, and so they call her by the name of *good Queen Bess;* when at the same time she has the character

ter in history of being " vain, proud, im-
" perious, and in some cases cruel; and
" that she entertained spies in all the houses
" of the nobility, encouraged informers,
" introduced the use of tortures, enacted a
" a great number of penal laws, and by the
" terror of her suspicion, which was ge-
" nerally fatal to the object, drove many
" gentlemen into excile, that she might per-
" secute them to confiscation, and enjoy
" their estates. Her choleric disposition
" prompted her to revile foreign Ambas-
" sadors, in the grossest terms, to insult her
" Ministers and subjects in the most abu-
" sive language, and even to chastise her
" female attendants with her own hand.
" On such occasions she used to utter oaths
" and imprecations in the most vulgar
" stile; and the ladies of her court did not
" scruple to follow her example. Her
" great art consisted in cajoling her Parlia-
" ment and people with the most flattering
" caresses." So far Smollet. And Guthrie
says, *That she was the most compleat hypocrite
that ever existed*; and he likewise says, *that
she did the blackest deed that ever stained
the pen of history:* namely, in the murder
of the most amiable Mary Queen of Scots.
And as to her want of modesty, look in
the above historians, where you will see her

lewd

lewd behaviour *with the Earl of Leicester, Essex, and the rest.*

Another thing which falls under my confideration, is that of Proteftants being taught to call all men who revert to the old ancient way of worfhip, *turncoats,* &c. at the fame time not confidering how by that appellation they are condemning themfelves, and the firft promoters of their new faith. For inftance, fuppofe that any of us had lived in this country in the days of *Edward* or *Elizabeth,* what a number of people fhould we have feen feduced, and turning from the ancient way of ferving God, and deferting the religion of their Chriftian anceftors; all whom were certainly *turncoats* in the ftricteft fenfe, and then it will follow that all thofe who practife and imitate their faid alterations muft be fo likewife; that is, muft have their religion or coat of the wrong fide outwards; therefore, if a man happening to be born of thefe parents, fhould after mature deliberation alter his coat, and wear it on the right fide; fure then he is far from deferving the name of turncoat. Thus out of your own mouths will I judge ye, and fhew plainly that the very expreffions which you now ufe to vindicate your practice of religion, are what will prove you to be in an error. For if (as you fay) men ought to be contented to live

live in that religion which they were born in, and not to turn their coats: then the first Reformers were guilty of a breach of this rule, in striving to overthrow the Ancient religion of this kingdom: and thus they stand convicted by you their children, who in imitation of them, *have turn'd your coats so oft*, that you have at last almost turned all religion out of this land, and introduced in its stead, Atheism, Deism, Freethinking, and all that dismal catalogue of Heterodox and impious sects, which now cover this Isle, as a part of that *innumerable army of Gog and Magog*, which St. John said *should deceive the Nations*.

Before I leave off, I must inform you (agreeable to a promise I made to some of my friends) what is the danger of Heresy, and who are Hereticks, and who are not, because but few Protestants know it.

Now Heresy is a dangerous thing, because it is a work of the flesh, and St. Paul says, Gal. v. 20. " That they which do " them shall not inherit the kingdom of " God." And he elsewhere says, that " there is but one Lord, one faith, one bap- " tism, one God and Father of all." So there is but one true Church of Christ out of all the multitude that claim that name, nor but one true Church which Christ has promised to be with even unto the end of the world,

world, directing and guiding her unto all truth; and if so, all reasonable men, certainly should embrace the true Church, which is easily discovered by these marks, namely, she is one, and holy. Now here see, what the ancient Fathers of the Church say concerning those that are divided from the unity of Christ's Church, and I shall quote only from them to whose authority the Church of England oft refers: Beginning first with St. Augustine, who says in his Epistle xv. 2. *Whosoever is separated from this Catholic Church, how laudable soever he may think himself to live, shall be excluded from eternal life, and remain obnoxious to God's heavy wrath, as being guilty of the heinous crime of being divided from the unity of Christ*; and again he says [super Gest. Emerit] *Out of the Catholic Church an Heretick may have all things but salvation. He may have the sacraments, he may sing Hallelujah, he may answer Amen, he may keep the Gospel, he may have the faith and preach it: only salvation he cannot have.* And again he says, [August. de. Symb. ad. Catech. lib. 4, chap. 10.] *Neither shall he have God for his father who will not have the Church for his mother. It will nothing profit such a one, that he hath been orthodox (or sound) in his belief, done so many good works*

R 2 and

*and the rest.* Also St. Cyprian says, in his book of the Unity of the Church, *Do they think* (says he) *that Christ is amongst them when they are assembled? I speak* (says he) *of those which make assemblies out of the Church. No; although they were drawn to torments and execution, for the confession of the name of Christ; yet this pollution is not washed away: no, not with their blood. This inexplicable, and inexcusable crime of Schism is not purged away, even by death itself. That man cannot be a Martyr who is not in the Church.*

Also St. Chrysostom in one of his Homilies, [Hom 11. in Ephes.] tells us, *There is nothing doth so sharply provoke the wrath of God as the division of the Church; inasmuch as though we should have performed all other sorts of good things, yet we shall incur a punishment no less cruel, by dividing the unity and fulness of the Church, than those have done, who pierced and divided Christ's body.*

And St. Athanasius says, *Whosoever expects to be saved, must necessarily (before all things) assent to, and retain the Catholic faith; which, unless he preserves entire and inviolate (that is, entirely submits to it) without all question he shall perish everlastingly.* And again, at the end of the Creed, he says, *This is the Catholic Faith, which, except*

cept a man believe faithfully he cannot be saved. From all which it appears, that obstinate Hereticks are in a lamentable state, therefore all Heresies ought to be avoided.

And to let you see who are not, and who are Hereticks, I shall here quote St. Augustine again, who, in his Epist. xvi. 2. says, " They that defend their opinions (altho' " they be false and erroneous) with no " stubbornness, nor obstinacy, especially if " they be such, as themselves did not " broach by bold presumption, but receiv- " ed them of their wicked parents, and do " seek the truth warily and carefully, being " ready to be reformed, if they find it, such " are not to be reputed Hereticks." He only is an Heretick, who obstinately defends unsound and erroneous opinions, and those who have had the Catholick doctrine made plain and manifest unto them, but nevertheless still resist it, and chuse that which suits best with their depraved judgment; these are Hereticks.

The people that scarce know that there are any other Pastors, or any other Church than their own, or who pretend not to pass their judgment on other Religions, their simplicity will, we hope, excuse them, by reason of their inability to examine scripture and churches, and so by invincible ignorance will, we presume, escape the malignity

nity of Schism. But then, those who have a capacity, and can read and judge of spiritual authority, and who it is they owe their subjection to, and yet make so ill a use of what God has given them, as to pervert scripture, and judge of the sense of it both for themselves and their Pastors, such are in a dangerous Schism: because they usurp an authority which the scripture says belongs not unto them.

Lastly, I shall set down a few short, but general heads, which I think sufficient to keep any one in the Catholick Faith, especially those who make it their study to serve God, and gain Heaven.

First, the Antiquity, and long continuance of the Catholick Religion, which for so many ages has kept the distinguishing title of *Catholic, which no other Religion ever could attain to.*

Secondly, The uninterrupted succession of Bishops, which they derive from *the Apostles themselves*, which succession no other Religion has any just claim unto.

Thirdly, The multitudes who always were of that persuasion, *which shews the universality of it.*

Fourthly, The great consent and agreement of all Catholicks with one another in what is affirmed to be points of faith, *which unity none else have.*

Fifthly,

Fifthly, Their being inftrumental in converting divers nations to Chriftianity, when none of all the Proteftants that ever departed from her faith, can fo much as fay, *that they ever converted one nation, or town, or village.*

Sixthly, Their piety and aufterity in their religious orders, and the celibacy of their Priefts, fhews that by their thus denying themfelves the moft pleafing things of this life, they *diligently ftrive to make Almighty God their friend.*

Seventhly, The riches of their churches, the feverity of their fafts, and other exterior obfervances, fhew it moft plain that it is not the filthy lucre of this world, nor the pleafing dreams of the voluptuous, that their Religion teaches them to aim at; but contrarywife, to pay their higheft acknowledgments to their Creator and Redeemer, in beautifying and enriching his temples that are dedicated to his fervice; and to mortify their paffions, and to bring their bodies into fubjection, fo that they may be enabled to ferve God in the beauty of holinefs.

Laftly, The wicked and unjuft laws that have been made againft Catholicks, by fome of their adverfaries who have departed from them, and the indirect methods that have been ufed by fome to deceive the ignorant and

and unlearned, in order to draw them into Herefy and Schifm, is enough, I think, to make any man who is not quite blinded by fuperftition, to fly from all upftart *new faiths*, and feek and ftand in the " good " old way, which all his noble anceftors " formerly trod in." For thofe old fafhion Chriftians were the men that did all the great deeds that this degenerate age has to boaft on. For by Catholicks was " Mag- " na Charta fettled;" by them was the law made " that every man fhould be try'd by " a jury of his Peers;" by them was won the glorious victories " of Creffy, Agin- " court, and Poictiers," and by them were Englifhmen made GREAT *and* FREE. For " Penal laws, and paper money," were not by them efteemed, to be either " the fafe- " ty, or riches of the nation." In their time the Penal laws were fo few, that the liberty of the fubject was not at all hurt thereby, and " paper credit was not fo " much as known." Awake, therefore, oh may Countrymen! and by a timely return to your duty, pluck yourfelves out of that labyrinth of confufion, in which you have been fo long bewildered, and confider that nothing will avail you, " if you lofe " your own fouls, for what fhall a man " give in exchange for his foul?" So here I conclude this part, with wifhing that England

land may once more be blessed with the knowledge of the *truth*; with real liberty; with riches that are not imaginary; and with every other good thing of which she stands in need: and may the blessing of Heaven attend all those who wish her prosperity.

# The APPENDIX.

IN which I desire the reader to take notice, that the following pages are not intended to affront the teachers of any Religion, but only by way of antidote to my friends against all upstart new faiths.

And first, I beg leave to observe how Luther in the year 1519, when he had began to broach his errors, wrote to Pope Leo the Xth. *that he did not design in any wise to meddle with his, or the power of the Church of Rome; and that if he would oblige his adversaries to the like injunction, he would bind himself to perpetual silence.* So little did he deem this Reformation necessary, which hath since been so much boasted of. In 1520 he spoke somewhat higher; because the contest grew warmer: and in another letter he wrote to the Pope, he says, *I abhor disputes; I'll attack no man, nor be myself attacked. If I be, having Jesus Christ for my Lord and Master, they shall not go unanswered. As for recanting what I have said, let no man look for it: your Holiness with one word may finish all these contests by bringing the cause to your own tribunal,*

*bunal, and imposing silence on both sides.* He also wrote to Charles the Vth, *That he would be an humble and obedient son of the Catholic Church, even to death; and promised to hold his peace if his enemies would but let him.* But this affair had made too great a noise to be huddled up so: therefore Luther was tried and condemned; and instead of the obedience he promised, he forgot all submission, and flew out to the most low and indecent expressions, and immediately set up for a preacher sent by an extraordinary mission; though, says he, *After I had got the better of all the arguments which were opposed against me, one remained still which with extreme difficulty, and great anguish, I could scarce conquer, even with the assistance of Jesus Christ: namely, that we ought to hear the Church.* Thus grace, as I may say, with reluctance abandoned this unhappy man, who afterwards kept no temper, but sallied out into those expressions that should scandalize his disciples, but they being above it were encouraged by them, and by hearing catched the contagious phrensy; and numbers looked upon Luther as an hero, a man from Heaven; and when they heard him defy threats and dangers, and say, *Though he absconded for a while, the Devil knew full well, it proceeded not from fear,* &c. At these brutish words

words his disciples discovered *something supernatural, a divine ardour, a celestial instinct, and the enthusiasm of an heart inflamed with the glory of the gospel.* And the success which attended Luther's boldness was deemed miraculous; and soon he assumes the tone of a prophet, and after admonishing, threatens to pray against his opposers, and assures them, *His prayers will not be Salmoneus's thunder, no empty rumbling in the air:* No, says he, *Luther's voice is not stop'd so, and I wish your Highness find it not to your cost; my prayer is an impregnable bulwark, more powerful than the Devil himself, see in his Epist. to G. Duke of Saxony, tom. 2. f. 491.* After this he addresses himself to the Pope in such a fulsome manner, that if it were not for shewing the furies that possessed this *grand Reformer*, I should be ashamed to transcribe them, which began thus to the Pope, *My little Paul, my little Pope, my little Ass; walk gently, the frost has made it slippery: thou'lt break a leg, thou'lt befoul thyself, and they'll cry out, O, the Devil! how the little Ass of a Pope has befouled himself!* Pardon me, O ye readers, and if you be followers of Luther's doctrine, reap some advantage of your own confusion at the sight of these foul ideas; for spite and malice

lice was the occasion of all he taught, as witness where he faith, *To spite the Papists, I am determined to believe that the bread and wine remain:* see his book to the Vaudois. If it was not that people once prejudiced believe every thing that a bold preacher dares tell them, one would think, that after seeing the foregoing and following expressions of Luther, a man might, without much difficulty, open his eyes, and see that this new gospel preacher aimed at nothing but dominion over men's consciences; for in full audience he told them, saying, " Moreover, if you pretend to continue " doing things by these common de- " liberations, I will unsay without demur- " ring, all that I have writ or taught: " I'll make my recantation and leave you. " Remember I have said it, and after all, " what hurt will the Popish Mass do you?" Now one would think he dreamt, when he reads such things in Luther's works, printed at Wirtemburgh; and in amaze say, How difficult a thing is it for a man to see, and confess his error! Alas, how horrible is the sight! that mankind by artifice should be deceived, obeying the dictates of the spirit of error, insomuch, that all the examples that truth itself can collect, are useless in this unbelieving age, where the preacher has finished that prejudice which

the

the nurse began; which has rendered numbers incapable of discerning the truth, causing them easily to be led by those who preach the delusions of their own frantick brains: and although there is no error but what contradicts itself, yet men possessed with strong prejudice, strive whatever they can to avoid seeing such glaring contradictions, and if this cannot be done, they then look upon it with a prepossession that does not allow them to form a right judgment of it, and think to fence against it by soothing themselves with frothy reasoning and fine words, than dazzled with some specious principle to which they are strongly wedded, they resolve never to forsake it; and being thus prepossessed with blind determination, they boldly lead the van, and draw after them the giddy vulgar, without being willing, or able to understand, (as says the Apostle, 1 Tim. i. 7.) *either what they themselves say, nor whereof they affirm.* This it is that constitutes all the new opinions that are amongst us, and this is the pit that all who fly from truth fall into.

Zuinglius, another of the pretended Reformers, whose doctrine gained great footing in this Island, has the character of a daring man, whose fire surpassed his learning; who, with great presumption, in his profession of faith, places Hercules, The-

seus

seus, Aristides, Antigonus, Numa, Camillus, the Catos, and Scipios, pell mell with Jesus Christ, and the saints, although some were the heroes themselves whom the idolatrous Romans worshipped; and Numa was the father of the Roman idolatry; and notwithstanding this presumption of him in furnishing Heaven with false Gods, yet this man passed for one of those who was extraordinarily sent by God to reform his church, and shew men the direct road to Heaven.

Oecolampadius, another defender of the figurative sense, who being tired with celibacy left his monastry, and like the rest of the Reformers married a young girl whose beauty he was smitten with. " This being
" the way (as said Erasmus) which they
" chused to mortify themselves;" and he testifies, " that he could not but admire
" these new Apostles who were sure to quit
" the solemn profession of celibacy to take
" wives, whereas the true Apostles of our
" Saviour, according to the tradition of all
" the Fathers, to the end they might attend
" to God and the gospel only, left their
" wives to embrace celibacy." And, again, he says, " It seems as if the Reformation
" aimed at nothing else than stripping a
" few Monks of their habits, and marrying
" a parcel of Priests; but the people at this
" time were so charmed with novelty, and
" the

" the much learning and sweet eloquence
" of the Reforming-Preachers, that were it
" possible (says the same writer) and would
" God have permitted it, it were capable
" of seducing even the elect. God put them
" to this trial, but his promises and truth
" upheld the simplicity of the Church's
" faith against human reasoning." Nevertheless numbers were drawn away by these blasphemers, and although their blasphemy was so conspicuous, yet men either could not or would not see it, although Luther decided, " That God's prescience renders free-
" will impossible; that Judas for that rea-
" son could not help betraying his master;
" that all that happens to man, whether
" good or evil, happens by pure and inevi-
" table necessity; that it is God who ope-
" rates in man all the good and evil that is
" done by him, and makes man guilty of
" damnation by necessity; that David's a-
" dultery is no less the work of God than
" the vocation of St. Paul." Lastly, " That
" it is no more unworthy of God to damn
" the innocent, than to forgive, as he does,
" the guilty." And Luther suffers no reply on this head, but says, " You that hear me
" never forget that I am the man who thus
" teaches, and without any new enquiry
" submit to this word." And this shall

suffice

suffice for a specimen of Luther's blasphemy.

Now hear whether Calvin is not as compleat a blasphemer as Luther; who says as follows: "That Adam could not avoid his
"fall, and was nevertheless guilty, because
"he fell voluntarily; that it was ordained
"by God and comprized in his secret de-
"crees." Furthermore he says, "That a
"hidden counsel of God is the cause of
"hardness of heart; that we must not de-
"ny God willed and decreed the defection
"of Adam, since he does all he wills; that
"this decree, he must confess, raises hor-
"ror, yet after all it cannot be denied but
"God foresaw the fall of man, because he
"had ordained it by his own decree; that
"we ought not to use the word permission,
"since it is an express order; that the
"will of God makes the necessity of things,
"and all he hath willed happens necessari-
"ly; that it was for this reason Adam fell by
"an order of God's providence, and because
"God had so judged it fitting, although he
"fell through his own fault; that the re-
"probate are inexcusable, although they
"cannot shun the necessity of sinning, and
"that this necessity befals them by God's
"appointment; that God speaks to them
"but on purpose to make them more deaf;
"that he places light before their eyes but

"on purpose to blind them; that he ap-
"plies sound doctrine to them, but on pur-
"pose to render them the more insensible;
"that he sends them remedies but to the
"end they may not be cured." Beza, also,
another Grand Reformer, refers "all sins
"to the will of God as their first cause."
Thus the Reformers in general taught, that
God drove on wicked men to enormous
crimes, and made the Author of all good,
the cause of all evil. Now whether these
men were sent by God to reform mankind,
and teach them his will, directing them into all truth, I shall not trouble myself to say,
only leave every man who has sense, to
judge for himself. Nevertheless, it is strange
to find that these great men who called
themselves Reformers, agreed in nothing so
much as they did in blasphemy, for in every
other thing they will bear eternal testimony
one against another, which will plainly shew
to those who are unprejudiced, how unhappily
they usurpt the title of Reformers, and also
point out, that the very method which they
took for the correction of abuses, could tend
to nothing but the subversion of Christianity. Now as the pretended Reformers could
not agree among themselves, what greater
absurdity than for each to set laws to mankind, all of them pretended to appeal to
the pure word of God, but each believed
himself

himself the true interpreter, and to vindicate himself cried out, *Why it's as clear as the sun, open your eyes and you need do no more*; and yet each contradicted the other. And thus it is when men forsake the unity of the Catholick Church, they are for ever in eternal disagreement, which proves that the Reformation was an evil thing; their disagreement amongst themselves is the cause of shewing it in its proper colours, yet a Church of England man cries out and says, I understand the scriptures a-right; the Presbyterian says the same; the Anabaptist declares that his Church is the true Interpreter; the Quaker affirms the self-same thing; and after all, when you come to hear their interpretations summed up, they are as different as light from darkness, and each supports a contrary faith, from this contrariety of interpreting: and yet each persuades himself that he is certain of the true exposition, and that he goes by scripture, and makes that his rule and guide, whilst he contradicts every other reformed Church's doctrine in the world, all which pretend at the same time to go by scripture as well as he, although they all contradict one another, and yet the scripture is not contradictory although all they understand it so, therefore it is plain that the mistake is in the people, and not in the scriptures; and that their contradictions arife from their pride and prefumption in expounding, and not from any difference in Holy Writ. All men who have offered to eftablifh any new fect of Chriftians, have undertook to deliver the true fenfe of the fcriptures in every point as it was underftood in the primitive Church. Although in the multiplicity of the undertakers, and contrariety of their doctrines, they have plainly fhewed the world that whatever their pretenfions were, in reality they had no knowledge of what was taught in the primitive Church; but that every one laboured to preach up and propagate their own fentiments and opinions, calling them *the doctrines of the Apoftles and firft ages of Chriftianity*, and this they themfelves have demonftrated to all mankind, for thofe who have recommended themfelves as Reformers, and as men fent from God to inform the world what was the doctrine of the Apoftles, and the belief of the primitive times, have all groffly contradicted one another, fome having preached up infant baptifm, and others cried it down; fome have maintained confubftantiation in the Sacrament, and others denied it; fome were for free-will and predeftination, and others againft it; fome afferted epifcopacy, and others oppofed it, &c.

Now

Now it is plain that all these contradictions, could not possibly be the doctrine of the Apostles; for where can any one find them preaching up baptism and no baptism; consubstantiation and no consubstantiation; free-will and no free-will, &c. And if it was not the doctrine of the Apostles that these teachers did preach, then they may be justly looked upon rather as Impostors than Reformers, who were not sent by God, but pushed on by their own pride and presumption, and to this they themselves have given testimony by their giving one another the lye in their preaching and expositions of Holy Writ: for amongst so many contradictions some must necessarily be false; and what better must the assertors of them be, than false Apostles and false Prophets? Such as interpreted the Holy Scriptures according to their own sense and judgment, and presumptuously preached it up for the sense of Christ and his Apostles. All of them it is true promise great things, crying aloud to the gaping croud, I am right, I interpret the scriptures according to the faith of the Apostles, and on this foundation I stand.

And yet what is to their eternal confusion, they all contradict one another; and not one of them has ever been able to give a miracle as a mark to distinguish his apostolical

ſtolical doctrine by; whilſt the Catholic faith has been eſtabliſhed every where by miracles, as witneſſeth the Converſion of this Iſland by St. Auguſtine, and the unity of all Catholicks in points of faith, is a ſtanding proof in oppoſition to all contradictory doctrines, that ſhe is that *one Holy Catholick Church* which all men ought to be in communion with. And the ſtupendous myſteries of the Catholick Religion ſhews its divine origin.

Whilſt the contradictions, and ridiculous abſurdities of all Proteſtants, prove to a demonſtration, that the God of all power and wiſdom had no hand in making the model. Who but God could have invented or introduced as an article of faith, the real preſence in the holy Euchariſt? All the powers upon earth could never have perſuaded men to receive it, nay, and what is more, the greateſt mortal, or ſet of mortals in the world, durſt not ſo much as have propoſed it; whilſt the groſs contradictions in the Proteſtant ways of receiving the Sacrament, and their ridiculous methods of defineing what it is, proves the abſurdity of their faiths.

Again, had not Auricular confeſſion been taught by Chriſt and his Apoſtles, who could have introduced it as an article of faith? Man would never have taught ſuch a disagreeable doctrine to human nature; especially if he had intended to make any converts to his Religion, consequently had not the Sacrament of penance had God for its parent, such a mortifying doctrine had never been introduced as an Article of Faith.

For look into all the new Religions that have sprung up among Protestants, and you will find little introduced but what sooths the passions, and instead of mortification and penance, you hear the cry of liberty, the glorious liberty of the gospel, which has so bewitched the vulgar, that all obedience to pastors is now called slavery, and to submit to be directed by the Bishops and Priests of Christ's Church is by Protestants termed being Priest-ridden; which has made such an intire riddance of humility and obedience, that even tinkers, coblers, and chimney-sweepers, now pretend to be as able to conduct and teach their neighbours the road to Heaven, as the greatest Pope, or learnedst Bishop in the Universe.

Besides, the boldness of Luther, in cutting off from scripture whatsoever did not suit with his notions, adds also to the infamy of his followers, and shews that licentiousness and independency had the greatest hand in the Reformation. Melancton, Luther's disciple owns the same when in writing

ing to him, he says, *Our associates do not dispute for the gospel, but who shall govern.* And this striving for mastery is what always happens when the yoke of lawful authority is cast off, and then those who cause an insurrection under the colour of liberty, too oft turn tyrants themselves. Oh! how ought all thinking mankind to take warning at others pride, and trembling, humble themselves, acknowledging that in man there is a profound source of pride and error, and that his weaknesses are unfathomable; for from hence has sprang the spiritual power of Princes, and all other abominations which have endeavoured to strip Christianity of all its mysteries, and change it into a sect of Philosophy wholly adapted to the senses: in a word, it is pride that has introduced most of the implements of seduction in this, and all other nations, which have produced such monsterous opinions, which makes it hard to be believed that men could have been so strangely infatuated, had not experience taught us that God sets to man's proud mind, examples of the blindness he may fall into, when abandoned to himself.

I will here add a proof or two how Protestants discredit themselves with regard to the doctrine they draw from the revelations; and that is concerning antichrist, whom they
call

call the Pope, look into Revelations the 9th, verse the first, *And the fifth Angel blew the trumpet, and I saw a star which was fallen from Heaven unto the Earth, and to him was given the key of the bottomless pit.* Now the note in the Protestant Bible, printed in London in the year 1599, hath these express words, *This authority chiefly is committed to the Pope, in sign whereof he beareth the keys in his arms.* Now how far these wise translators were right in their explanations, I shall not presume to decide, but it must be for some other reasons that Protestants paint St. Peter with the keys, and I can assure them this, that he was the first Pope that ever was in the world, and that all other Popes wear the keys as being his lawful successors; therefore, the gross absurdity of this note I shall take no further notice of, but proceed to shew what the same wise gentlemen gather from these words of the 7th verse of the eleventh chapter, *The beast that cometh out of the bottomless pit, shall make war against them, and shall overcome them, and kill them;* that is the Pope (as they say in the notes) *which hath his power out of Hell, and cometh thence.* Now is there not great charity in these expressions? And again, the same notes say, *He sheweth how the Pope gaineth the victory, not by God's word, but by cruel war;*

U and

and as if slander and calumny were the main pillars on which is built the so much boasted Reformation, they proceed to define the meaning of these words in the sixteenth chapter, and 2d verse, *And there fell a noisome and grievous sore upon the men which had the mark of the beast*, which in their notes they say, *This was like the sixth plague of Egypt, which was sores and boils, or pox; and this reigneth commonly among Canons, Monks, Friars, Nuns, Priests, and such filthy vermin, which bear the mark of the beast.* And again, they say in the note on the 13th verse, *That is a strong number of this great Devil the Pope's Ambassadors, which are ever croaking like frogs, and come out of Antichrist's mouth, because they should speak nothing but lyes, and use all manner of crafty deceits, to maintain their rich Euphrates against the true Christians.* Alas! if such vile and scandalous stuff as this is becoming a Protestant's Bible, much good may the choice and decent language do them: but these explaining gentlemen do not stop here, but like men who are above shame, they endeavour to explain the 4th verse of the seventeenth chapter, in the following manner: *This woman is Antichrist, that is the Pope, with the whole body of his filthy creatures*, (as is expounded in verse the 18th) *that instead of doing homage to Christ Jesus,*

*are*

are *cast into a reprobate sense to serve Antichrist, and to dedicate themselves wholly unto him whose beauty only standeth in outward pomp and impudence, and craft like a strumpet.* Pardon me, Catholicks, for these digressions, and take warning, O ye Protestants, at the errors of your leaders, and reap some small advantage from their confusion; who to support themselves were drove to such mean shifts as these, in order to deceive the unwary; for in what does the Pope resemble Antichrist? who according to St. Paul, 2 Thess. second chapt. and 4th verse, *Opposeth and exalteth himself above all that is called God, or that is worshipped*; and according to the Revelations, *shall continue but a short time.*

Now Antichrist is, and must be a single person, so that all Popes cannot be Antichrist; and if one ever had been, it is surprising that the Protestants never can tell which is that Pope that they ought to praise God evermore for the destruction of, as they uncharitably express in their note on the 4th verse of the 19th chapter of Revelations.

And how the present Pope sheweth himself to be God, *denying the Father and the Son, as Antichrist*, (see 1 John, ii. 22.) I know not, unless Protestants understand him to be such when he offers up the sacri-

fice

fice of the mass. And who does not see how the Pope shews himself to be God in that solemn office, where *first he exalts himself above every thing, by confessing his sins with the people, and intreating all the saints and his brethren to beg forgiveness for him*; afterwards he declares, *he hopes for this forgiveness, not through his own merits; but through the bounty and grace, and in the name of Jesus Christ our Lord?* Now let me ask any reasonable man, if this is not a strange kind of Antichrist, that obliges all his adherents to place their hope in Jesus Christ, and for ever to assert his divinity? Sure it is, for Antichrist, as saith the scripture, *is not of God, and denieth that Christ is come in the flesh*, 1 John, iv. 3.

And into as great a contradiction are Protestants fell, in relation to the perpetuity and visibility of Christ's Church; for although it is plain that they join'd to no Church that ever was before them, yet they teach in their Confession of Faith, first made at Ausburgh, *That there is a holy Church which must eternally subsist*; and again they say, *The Church is an assembly of saints, wherein the gospel is rightly taught, and the Sacraments rightly administred.*

Now after people have allowed this, how dare they accuse the Church of error, either in doctrine, or in the administration of

of the Sacraments? for if she teaches the gospel rightly, and administers the Sacraments rightly, how is it possible to accuse her of teaching errors in points of faith? therefore, according to the aforesaid definition of the Church, it is impossible she should teach errors: and thus the Protestants who accuse her of erring, carry in their Confession of Faith their own condemnation. And the Helvetick Confession defines the Church in this manner, saying, *Which hath been always, which is, and which shall ever be the assembly of the faithful, and of the saints who know God, and serve him by the word and the Holy Ghost:* and afterwards they say, *That lawful and true preaching is her chief mark*; whence they conclude that the Churches which are deprived of these marks, " although they boast
" the succession of their Bishops, their unity
" and their antiquity, do not belong to the
" Church of Jesus Christ, nor can salvati-
" on any more be had out of the Church,
" than out of the Ark; if you will have
" life you must not separate yourself from
" the true Church of Jesus Christ." Thus far this solemn Confession made by Protestants:—Now I beg it may be observed, that if Protestants cannot shew plainly that visible Church to which they joined themselves,

felves, then it will remain an uncontested truth, that from their own confession they are not the Catholick Church of Jesus Christ, and therefore are to be avoided, because they themselves own " if you will " have life, you must not separate yourself " from the true Church of Jesus Church." And the Ausburgh confession is very plain touching its visibility, for it says, " We " never have dream't that the Church was " a platonick city not to be found on earth: " we say that the church exists; that in it " there are true believers, and men truly " just spread over all the universe: we add " to this, its marks, the pure gospel, and " the Sacraments; and it is such a church, " that is properly the pillar of the truth." Here now is a fair acknowledgment made by the first Protestants, in their own confession of faith, that the church of Christ is really existing, really visible, and in which sound doctrine is really preached, and the Sacraments really administred as they ought to be. Therefore, as these things were actually allowed by Protestants, at their first appearance upon earth, is it not somewhat strange that none of their descendants can shew us which was the church and society of pastors and people, wherein sound doctrine had always been preserved; that Luther, the first grand Reformer, joined himself felf unto: Alas! that people will love error rather than truth, when at the fame time, nothing in all the world can be more plain than this, "That there was not any one church, little nor great before Luther's coming, that was of his fentiments;" and the fame may be faid of *Calvin, Zuinglius,* &c. Befides, as there had been always a true church, if thefe Reformers had found it, they might then eafily have fhewn what they are all fo much at a lofs to difcover, namely, their great Bifhop who firft authorized and deputed them to preach, &c. for how can they preach except they be fent? "But as the Reformation cannot produce one paftor of the true church, to which they pretend they joined, that did confecrate;" fo neither can they find any people that could elect, which implies that it is not the truth which thofe bold men *(called Reformers)* came to preach, and confequently their doctrine ought to be abhored; for if it cannot be made plainly appear that Luther and Zuinglius' doctrine and faith was abfolutely known and practifed by fome fet of people, before they appeared to preach it, then nothing can be more true that they did not join themfelves to the catholic church of Chrift, which every chriftian in the Apoftles creed profeffes to believe: and as their faith and doctrine was utterly unknown

unknown before their times, therefore it is certain that it could not be truth, becaufe *Chrift promifed to be with his church always*; and Proteftants own that for that reafon fhe cannot help but be vifible, and that fhe always teacheth truth: now the confequence is plain, that whoever departeth from her doctrine, but for one moment, does by fo doing declare his enmity to truth; and until the friends of the Reformation can fhew that church which their firft directors joined unto, and wherein truth had always been preached, they muft of neceffity ftand convicted before all men who have eyes to fee, or ears to hear. Suffer me to afk, " How " it can be imagined that all the paftors of " Chrift's church could at one time fall into " error, and deceive all the faithful " throughout the whole world?" And if they could not all be deceived at one time, (which indeed it is impoffible they fhould) then Proteftants of different faiths fhould fhew where was the true church that they joined unto; or elfe they may be looked upon as mere upftarts, whofe firft teachers were no more than hardy innovators, who defpifed church authority, and chofe rather an unbridled licentioufnefs in all matters of religion; and their followers at laft grown giddy with changes, are become fo ready and willing to receive errors, that a man

need

need only to have but impudence enough to preach, and then let his doctrine be never so wicked or ridiculous, yet in this land of learning he is sure to find followers; and this is the source from whence has sprung such confusion in religion, in this island; and this is the consequence of subjecting the church to the world, learning to ignorance, and faith to the magistrate; but the union of Churches cannot depend on the will of Princes, nor can the learning of the Fathers submit to that of the Weaver, the Tinker, and Cobler; neither will the Catholick Church of Christ ever depend upon any other support, but the promise of her founder, who not only knew what he promised, but also is able to perform it; therefore *the gates of Hell* (that is error and darkness) *shall never prevail against her.*

If after all I have said it should be urged by a member of that Church in which I was educated, that the orders of their priests and deacons are valid, because they are established by a decree of Parliament; there is a doubt then arises, that had not the Parliament made such decrees, the ordination of their whole clergy would have been dubious. But these decrees are not only a salve for ordination, but for the sacrilegious rapine that was made on the sacred and inviolable treasure of the Church, which also is called *Reformation*; and *the re-establishing of evangelical purity:* but a thinking man would imagine it impossible for a nation to arrive at such a pitch as to discover innocence in deeds equally perverting all laws human and divine; for shall it be *a damning sin to rob man, and evangelical purity to rob God of the things dedicated to his service?* Or shall those who have *invaded openly the devotions of other men, and took from God and from his Church, what they never gave unto it, even the lands and livings thereof;* yea, *(as Sir Harry Spellman, who was a Protestant, in his* De non Temerandis Ecclesiis, *page* 8, *fol. edit.) the Churches themselves?* Shall those, I say, be called Reformers of Christ's Church? No, God forbid; for if it was a sin to make the house of God a house of merchandise; certainly, then it cannot be *innocence,* nor *evangelical purity,* to make merchandise of the house of God itself; but rather it must (as Sir H. Spellman says in page 9, of the aforesaid work) *be a fearful and most inhuman sin!* and as he says in page 17, *if it were so heinous a fact in Annanias, to withhold part of his own goods, which he pretended he would give unto God, how much more* (says he) *is it in us, presumptuously to reave that from God that others have already dedicated and delivered unto him.* Solomon saith, *he that robbeth*

*his*

his father and his mother, and faith it is no
fin, is the companion of a murderer, or him
that destroyeth. But he that purloineth the
things of God, robbeth his father; and he
that purloineth the things of the Church, robbeth his mother; and therefore that man is a
companion of the destroyer. With what face
canst thou expect an inheritance from Christ
in Heaven, that defraudeth Christ in his inheritance here on earth.—Therefore give unto
Cæsar the things that are Cæsar's, and unto
God the things that are God's. So far this
learned Protestant could discern it to be sinful to do as the first Reformers did in this
island. Therefore, as the Reformation was
conceived in sin, what else can it produce
but iniquity? for which manifest reason,
let all those who wish to gain Heaven,
strive upon a surer foundation, by joining
unto that Church *which is founded on a rock,
against which the gates of Hell* (that is error
and darkness) *shall not prevail.*

I shall here endeavour to answer a few
formidable questions asked by Protestants,
and then proceed to ask a few.

Protestants ask, whether the Pope be
infallible? This I allow is taught by Cardinal Bellarmin; but the Church requires
no assent to such a papal infallibility, nor
does the *formulæ* of faith, set forth by Pope

Pius IV. collected out of the Council of Trent, oblige any to make such profession; neither has the Pope's infallibility any place in any of our catechisms : nay, it is so far from being the faith of the Church, that twelve eminent Catholick Universities, and numbers of Bishops, Archbishops, and Cardinals write professedly against it, without ever being censured by the Church; nay, so far is the Church from looking upon Popes as infallible, that she has in a general Council deposed two, viz. Benedict the XIIIth, and Gregory the XIIth, and afterwards elected Alexander the Vth into their place; and the said Council declares, that all persons whatever, and amongst others the very Pope himself is bound to obey and be subject to their decrees, Coun. Const. Sess. 4 and 5. Conc. Bazil Sess 3. Therefore the Pope is not looked upon by Catholicks to be infallible : They also ask, Whether the Pope has a power to depose Princes, and absolve their subjects from their allegiance?

So Bellarmin asserts; but the Church requires no assent to any such doctrine, nor has it any place in her Catechise composed for instructing all in the faith of the Church. Numbers of Catholick Universities, and single writers oppose it as a doctrine new and erroneous : all the whole Gallican Church oppose

oppose it, therefore cannot be any point of faith, because both clergy and laity condemn it, and yet abide in the communion of the Catholick Church.

It is also asked, Whether it be lawful to desire the saints in Heaven to pray for us? And in answer to this, I shall quote Dr. Montague, Protestant Bishop of Chichester, and after of Norwich; who owns that the blessed in Heaven do recommend to God in their prayers, their kindred, friends, and acquaintance on earth: and having given his reasons for this, he inserts, that " this " is the common voice, with general con- " currence, without contradiction of reve- " rend and learned antiquity, for ought I " ever could read or understand : and I see " no cause or reason to dissent from them " touching intercession in this kind :" see his Treat. Invoc. of Saints, p. 103.

He owns, also, that it is no injury to the mediation of Christ to ask the saints to pray for us. " Indeed, I grant" (says he) " Christ " is not wronged in his mediation ; it " is no impiety to say, as they (of the " Romish Church) do ; Holy Mary, pray " for me ; holy Peter, pray for me." *And again he says,* " Could I come at them, or " certainly inform them of my state, with- " out any question or more ado, I would " readily and willingly say, holy Peter,
" blessed

"blessed Paul, pray for me; recommend
"my case to Christ Jesus our Lord. Were
"they with me, by me, in my kenning, I
"would run with open arms, and fall upon
"my knees, and with affection desire them
"to pray for me." And in p. 97. "I see
"no absurdity in nature, no incongruity
"unto analogy of faith, no repugnancy at
"all to sacred scripture, much less impiety,
"for any man to say, holy Angel guardi-
"an pray for me." And if so eminent a
Bishop could not but approve of praying to
saints and angels in the manner that Catholicks do, how comes it to pass that others
of less note do so vehemently cry it down?

It is likewise asked, Whether those in communion with the Roman Church are not idolaters in the worship of images, and especially in worshipping the cross on Good Friday?

To a Protestant it looks like idolatry, because we not only creep to it, but also bow down three times before it, and kiss it: but then we declare by these outward actions, we mean no more than to express that love and veneration which is due to the cross, as to other holy things, and to our Redeemer, who on that day died for us; and by it we pay an acknowledgment and thanksgiving to Christ, for preaching the gospel of salvation. It is no more than if being on

Mount

Mount Calvary, on Good Friday, we should prostrate ourselves, and on our knees kiss the ground where the cross stood. Now a grateful acknowledgment of faith and love is due to our Redeemer, in a more special manner on that day of our redemption: and if instead of our being on Mount Calvary, we humble ourselves in our churches, so as to creep upon the ground, and kiss the cross, so to express our acknowledgment of love to Christ; I cannot but hope that we may do it without being guilty of idolatry, however it may look to others, who through ignorance may take exception against it.

It is also asked, Whether the Roman Catholicks are not idolaters in worshipping bread and wine?

If we did worship bread and wine we might be termed idolaters; but as our church teaches, that the worship which we pay to the holy Eucharist is to be directed only to Christ, who is there present in an ineffable manner, and not to the elements of bread and wine: the charge of idolatry is groundless, for we detest and abhor the worshipping of bread and wine as much as Protestants can do, but when we believe Christ to be really present, we think it right to adore him; and that Christ is really and truly present on the altar after consecration, may be proved from the writings
of

of many eminent divines of the Church of England, whose testimonies I shall produce:—and first,

All those who made the catechise taught it, for they say, that the thing signified is the body and blood of Christ, which is verily and indeed taken and received by the faithful in the Lord's Supper; that is, the faithful are the communicants, who partake of the body and blood. Besides, the Minister says in the communion service, the body of our Lord, &c. and the blood of our Lord, &c.

In Queen Elizabeth's time, Mr. Hooker, in his Eccl. Pol. l. 5, teaches "that the "very person of our Lord himself, whole, "perfect, and entire, is received in a mysti-"cal manner."

In King James First's time, Bishop Andrews believed this point, who, in answer to Cardinal Bellarmine, says, "we believe "a true presence as much as you."

Bishop Mountague says, "there is in the "holy Eucharist a real presence."

Bishop Bilson says, "God forbid, that "we should deny that the flesh and blood "of Christ are truly present, and truly re-"ceived of the faithful at the Lord's "table."

Bishop Morton says, "The question is "not

" not concerning a real presence which Pro-
" testants do also profess."

Archbishop Laud gives his reason for paying reverence to the altar, " as being
" upon this account the greatest place of
" God's residence upon Earth."

Bishop Ken, in his Exposition, licenced 1685, says, " O God incarnate! how thou
" canst give us thy flesh to eat, and thy
" blood to drink; how thy flesh is meat in-
" deed; how thou, who art in Heaven, art
" present on the altar, I can by no means ex-
" plain; but I firmly believe it all because
" thou hast said it, and I firmly rely on thy
" love and thy omnipotence to make good
" thy word, though the manner of doing it
" I cannot comprehend."

Bishop Forbs, says, " Christ is present
" on the the holy table in an ineffable man-
" ner."

Bishop Taylor says, " We eat and drink
" the body and blood of Christ, that was
" broken and poured forth; for there is
" no other body, no other blood of Christ;
" but though it is the same we eat and
" drink, yet it is in another manner."
And before he says, " There is but one body
" of Christ, natural and glorified: but he
" that saith that body is glorified, which
" was crucified, says it is the same body,

" but

"but not after the same manner; and so it is in the Sacrament."

Mr. Thorndike says, "The elements are really changed from ordinary bread and wine, into the body and blood of Christ, mystically present as in a Sacrament; and that in virtue of consecration, and not by the faith of him that receives."

Dr. Parker, Bishop of Oxford, says, "As for the church of England, she agrees with the tradition of the catholic church, in asserting the certainty of the real presence, and the uncertainty of the manner of it, though the true account of it hath been miserably perplexed and disturbed by the oblique practices of the Sacramentarians."

Thus the church of England so far teaches that Christ is really present in the holy Eucharist, therefore where he is really present, he most certainly ought to be worshipped. And again, if the holy Eucharist be the body and blood of Christ, it cannot then be bread and wine; for our Saviour said, this is my body; and not, *in this* is my body; therefore it must be what his all powerful words make it: but it cannot be two substances at one and the same time, so if it is his true body it cannot be bread; but is converted or changed into the body and blood of Christ, which conversion or change the church calls Tranſubſtantiation. Now as this has always been the doctrine of the catholic church, that the bread and wine is converted, or changed, is it not ſtrange that people ſhould quarrel with her for framing a new word to expreſs this old point of faith? And although the word Tranſubſtantiation is not to be found in ſcripture, yet we underſtand by it no more than what the ſcripture teaches; namely, that after conſecration, what was before bread and wine, is, by the omnipotent power of God, converted or changed, and becomes the true body and blood of Chriſt, and this converſion or change being made only in the ſubſtance, which is inviſible, (the outward accidents or appearances remaining ſtill the ſame) the church hath thought convenient to expreſs the ſame by a new word, without ever altering what was before believed; which word is declared by her to be fit and proper, and by it we underſtand the very ſelf-ſame ſubſtantial preſence which all Catholicks ever believed in, and the very ſame change of ſubſtances that the church ever held.

Proteſtants alſo aſk, Whether the maſs is not an abomination? The maſs has this meaning, it is the performing that which Chriſt did at his laſt ſupper when he gave to his Apoſtles, and by them to their ſucceſſors,

cessors, power of consecrating the bread and wine into the body and blood of Christ, and commanded them to do what he had there done, in remembrance of his death and passion on the cross; it is also called a sacrifice, because Christ is offered in an unbloody manner under the forms of bread and wine, in testimony of God being the sovereign Lord of life and death; and in this sacrifice the virtue of Christ's passion is applied to Christians by means of this offering made unto God, in remembrance of Christ's being offered for our sins. And pray what is there in this that is abominable? or what new or strange thing is this mass? But minds prepossessed with prejudice condemn without due examination.

Then it is asked, Whether the Church of Rome does not act contrary to the command of Christ in forbidding the people the use of the cup? And whether the denial of the cup be not defrauding the laity?— Now we own that Christ said, *Drink ye all of this*; and that it was a plain command to those to whom he spoke, that is to the Apostles (and to their successors) whom he then made Priests, and gave them power to consecrate the elements as he had done: But as the power of consecrating, which Christ then gave to the Apostles, is not to be extended to the laity, so neither is the command of drinking, which he gave at the same time: many other commands also, were only given to the Apostles and their successors, as *Go, and teach all nations*; *Receive ye the Holy Ghost*; *Whose sins ye forgive, they are forgiven*, &c. with others of this kind, and none of them intended or directed to the people; we own the command is evident, but say that none can prove from evidence of scripture that this command was given to the laity: we also allow that it was the most general practice in the primitive church, for all to receive in both kinds even for 1100 years; but then we say that the church did not do this in obedience to any command of Christ, because if Christ had commanded it to be given under both kinds, then it would have been essentially necessary to salvation, for all to have received it in that manner; but we can prove from evident matter of fact, in the records of antiquity, that in the purest ages, it was the practice in many cases to give the communion in one kind only: as to the solitaries, to whom it was carried into the desart, to the sick, to persons on a journey, to infants, and to the abstemious; and for some time also, in some places, in the ordinary communion at church, as appears from S. Leo the Great, and S. Gelasius, who was his successor in the Roman See, being likewise wife taken notice of by Caſſander and Grotius. Now as this was practiſed in the ancient church, it is moſt evident, that it was judged then good and lawful to receive in one kind, which they could not have judged if Chriſt had left a command for all to receive in both; for if he had it muſt have been abhorred as a thing contrary to a plain precept of Chriſt. Hence, as the primitive church judged it good and lawful to receive in both kinds, ſo they judged it good and lawful (upon ſome motives and circumſtances) to receive in one kind; therefore it is plain that the manner of receiving, whether in both kinds, or one, was no matter of precept, but ſubject to difference of practice, according to circumſtances, and thus was reputed as a point of diſcipline, capable of change; and this is the very ſentiment of the preſent Roman Church, for we ſay that it is good to receive in one kind, and likewiſe that it is good to receive in both: it was the general practice formerly to receive in both kinds, and may be ſo again; but when there is danger of irreverence of giving the Sacrament in both kinds, there is no precept for ſo giving it, but it may lawfully and profitably be given in one. Now many leading men in the Church of England agree with us, that Chriſt has no where in ſcripture given command for all

to

to receive in both kinds: as Bishop Forbs, who owns the primitive practice of giving the communion in one kind in particular cases, and Bishop White, and Bishop Mountague, who say the authority for giving it in both kinds is rather from tradition than scripture: and so far do these learned men grant that it is not contrary to any precept to forbid the cup to the laity; therefore, as it is not a breach against the laws of God to receive in one kind, it is a point of discipline only, and may be altered as it has been before now, for in 1564, the Pope granted the use of the cup to the laity in Germany, hoping by that condescention to have united them to the church; and this he did by the power which the Council of Constance placed in him, *viz.* leaving it to the prudence of the Pope, to grant leave to any nation or people, of communicating in both kinds, as he should think reasonable.

Protestants also ask, Whether praying for the most wicked sinners be not a proof that Papists think purgatory a shelter for all crimes?

To this I answer, that as we believe that the very good and faithful servants of God go directly to Heaven, so we believe that sinners, who die without sincere repentance, go directly to Hell: but then as the inward

state

state of a dying christian is unknown to us, we suspend our judgment in this case, because God alone is judge, therefore we let our charity prevail, which supposing, and hoping the best, we pray for all such as die; knowing, that if the souls for which we pray are not capable of relief, yet our prayers will not be lost before God, who is the faithful rewarder of charity, though it happens to be misapplied, just as the apostolical salutation, peace be to this house, was not lost, even in a house where there was no son of peace; for that in this case, Christ promised the peace should return to their benefit, who made the prayer of peace for their neighbour. Thus our charity must be an innocent piety in praying for the souls departed; and if it is not commanded in scripture, I am sure it is not forbid. Now hear what some of the Bishops of the Church of England say on this head: and first observe what the late Duchess of York says in her paper.

I spoke severally to two of the best Bishops we have in England, (Sheldon, Archbishop of Canterbury, and Blandford, Bishop of Worcester) who both told me, there were many things in the Roman Church which it were much to be wished we had kept: as confession, which was no doubt commanded by God: that praying for the dead

dead was, was one of the antient things in chriſtianity: that for their parts they did it daily, though they would not own it: and before their time the learned Biſhop Forbs ſays, "Let not the antient practice
"of praying and making oblations for the
"dead, received throughout the univerſal
"Church of Chriſt, almoſt from the very
"time of the Apoſtles, be any more reject-
"ed by Proteſtants as unlawful, or vain.
"Let them reverence the judgment of the
"primitive church, and admit a practice
"ſtrengthened by the uninterrupted pro-
"feſſion of ſo many ages: and let them,
"as well in public as private, obſerve this
"rite, although not as abſolutely neceſſary,
"or commanded by the divine law, yet as
"lawful, and likewiſe profitable, and as al-
"ways approved by the univerſal church;
"that by this means, at length, a peace
"ſo earneſtly deſired by all learned and ho-
"neſt men, may be reſtored to the chriſti-
"an world." Again, he ſays, "The uni-
"verſal church has believed this practice,
"not only to be lawful, but beneficial to
"the ſouls departed, and has always moſt
"religiouſly obſerved it, as delivered, if
"not from the Apoſtles, at leaſt from the
"primitive Fathers; as is manifeſt in ma-
"ny places of their writings. Let it be
"granted that this cuſtom was always judg-

"ed

"ed lawful, and also profitable by pious antiquity, and most universally received at all times in the church." Thus this great Protestant Bishop asserts, who had taken pains to look into antiquity. Bishop Mountague also in his Appeal, c. 18. asserts a middle state, or third place, for he says positively, "That the souls of the righteous, before Christ's ascension, were not in Heaven, strictly taken, not in that Heaven which is now the receptacle of the righteous." Then in relation to the texts, which seem to restrain the state of departed souls either to Hell or Heaven, he says, "This is to be understood of the final state of souls after the day of judgment, when there will be no more than two conditions of souls everlastingly, viz. Heaven and Hell, and in this both churches agree." Appar. p. 135. Thus these Protestant Bishops teach to the confusion of the bigots of this age.

Next Protestants ask, Whether indulgences are not abominable, which either give leave to sin, or grant the pardon of past sins, for a sum of money?

This was the opinion I formerly had of indulgences; but since I became a Catholic, I have found that the Church of Rome grants no indulgences for leave to commit sins, nor pardons for past sins, but the very

time

same as has been practised in the purest ages of the church; and that is a remission of some part of canonical penance, or punishment due to sin. The occasion of their having been reputed pardons for sins, is, I presume, owing to their having been formerly called pardons; and as giving of alms has been generally one condition required for gaining indulgences, hence has it been thought that the pardon of sin was offered for money: but these are mistakes which Protestants but too oft make, for we believe that there is no pardon for sin, without true repentance, and an humble confession of sin; and if these do not precede, no indulgence can avail us in order to the remission of any punishment due to sin; therefore, if Protestants would argue fairly, they should state the case as we do believe, and not as they would make people think we believe; and then none could roar so loudly against indulgences as they now do.

Next Protestants ask, Whether it be not an abominable sacriledge in the Church of Rome, to go to men for the pardon of sin, whilst in so doing, they forsake God for man?

To this I answer, That Roman Catholicks believe as firmly as any Protestants, that there is no power but of God alone that can forgive sins: and that where God has made men the ministers of his power, there to go to such his ministers, is not to forsake God, or to seek any other power besides of God; but it is to comply with his ordinance, and consequently the direct way of seeking God; since doing his will is the most effectual way of going to him. *He that hears you, hears me*, are God's own words to his ministers. Now let us hear what the Church of England says concerning confession.

First, she advises it in the exhortation, giving warning of a communion; and more particularly a special confession is urged in the Rubrick at the visitation of the sick. But if confession is not requisite, why is the dying person to be then alarmed and troubled with it, when least capable to reflect upon his past life. Hear what Bishop Mountague says on this head:—" Private confession to
" a Priest is of very ancient practice in the
" church, of excellent use and benefit;
" being discretely handled. We refuse it
" to none, if men require it, if need be to
" have it; we urge and persuade it *in ex-*
" *tremis:* we require it in the case of per-
" plexity, for the quieting men disturbed
" and their consciences." Appeal, c. 32.

He elsewhere says, " That in the ordi-
" nation of Priests are these words, *Quorum*
" *remiseritis peccata*, whose sins you shall
 " forgive

"forgive they are forgiven;" and then he adds, "God ordinarily proceedeth, in re-
"mitting sin, by the churches act; and
"hence they have their parts in this work,
"and cannot be excluded; no more in this
"than in other acts, and parts of their
"function. And to exclude them, is (af-
"ter a sort) to wring the keys out of their
"hands to whom Christ has given them;
"is to cancel and make void this clause of
"*remiseritis*, as if it were no part of the
"sentence; to account of all this solemn
"sending, and inspiring, as if it were an
"idle and fruitless ceremony." Thus confession, which the Protestants of this age so much ridicule, is both taught and approved of by the Church of England and her Bishops; and therefore those who are in her communion, and yet speak against it, may certainly be deemed the introducers of new and strange doctrines.

Protestants ask, Whether it does not betray an intolerable pride and confidence in the Papists, to think they can do more than God requires at their hands, and more than is necessary, which they call works of Supererogation?

To this I answer, that this doctrine is not taught by the Catholick Church, for what we mean by works of Supererogation, is no
more

more than what any Proteſtant may approve, *viz.* That it is the performance of ſuch good works which God has not required of us by any precept; ſuch as it was in Mary Magdalene, when falling at the feet of Jeſus, in the Phariſee's houſe, ſhe anointed them with ointment, having firſt waſhed them with her tears, and wiped them with her hair. Repentance and love of Chriſt was commanded, but this her manner of expreſſing it, ſo acceptable to Jeſus, was not commanded, therefore was a work of Supererogation; and this is what we mean by the word, and no more.

The Proteſtant alſo aſks, Whether it be not a great cheat, to impoſe traditions on the world, for the doctrine of Chriſt, and the word of God?

It is true, we profeſs to receive traditions, but what traditions are theſe? Only apoſtolical and eccleſiaſtical traditions; that is, ſuch doctrines as were delivered by the apoſtles without being committed to writing, and being preſerved in the church in all ages, have been delivered down to our days; and we renounce all vain, and ſuperſtitious traditions of men, and receive none but ſuch as have a full and ſufficient teſtimony of their having been received from the apoſtles and pureſt ages of the church. The Church of England holds many traditions, as Infant Bap-

Baptism, the Apostles Creed, the Fast of Lent, the Lord's Day, the great festivals of Easter and Whit-Sunday; of not fasting on Sundays, of adoring towards the East, prosteration before the Altar, of signing the baptized with the Cross, &c. therefore, if Protestants will take the liberty of holding traditions which they believe to be primitive, surely they ought to allow Catholicks the same liberty of judging for themselves.

Many Protestants say that the Pope is Antichrist, and that Papists are idolaters; but some great men of the Church of England teach the contrary, as for instance, the learned Bishop Mountague, who says, " I pro-" fess, ingenuously, I am not of opinion " that the Bishop of Rome is personally that " Antichrist, nor yet that the Bishops of " Rome successively are that Antichrist " so spoken of," Gag. p. 74, 75. Mr. Thorndike, in his Just Weights and Measures, Char. 1st, says, " They that separate " from the Church of Rome, as idolaters, " are thereby schismaticks before God, and " in Char. 2d, Let not them who charge " the Pope to be Antichrist, and the Papists " idolaters, lead the people by the nose, to " believe that they can prove their supposi-" tion when they cannot."

Bishop Parker, speaking of this charge of idolatry, says, " So black a crime as this,
" that

" that is no less than renouncing God, is
" not lightly to be charged upon any party
" of Christians, not only because of the
" foulness of the calumny, but the barba-
" rous consequences that may follow from
" it, to invite and warrant the rabble, when-
" ever opportunity favours, to destroy the
" Roman Catholicks and their images, as
" the Israelites were commanded to destroy
" the Canaanites and their idols. But be-
" fore so bloody an indictment be preferred
" against the greatest part of christendom,
" the nature of the thing ought to be well
" understood. The charge is too big for
" a scolding word; and how inconsistent
" soever idolatry may be with salvation, I
" fear so uncharitable a calumny (if it prove
" one) can be of no less damnable conse-
" quence. It is a piece of inhumanity, that
" outdoes the savageness of the Cannibals
" themselves, and damns at once both body
" and soul. And yet after all we have no
" other ground for the bold conceit, than
" the crude and rash assertions of some po-
" pular divines, who have no other mea-
" sures of truth or zeal, but hatred to Po-
" pery; and therefore never spare for hard
" words against that church, and run up
" all objections against it into nothing less
" than atheism and blasphemy, of which
" idolatry is the greatest instance." Reas.

for

for Abrog. the Test. pag. 72, 73. Afterwards he is more particular in examining this charge, as consisting of these three heads:—

1. The worship of images.
2. Adoration of the host.
3. Invocation of saints.

Where he makes use of these words worthy to be considered; "But as to the
" first, the use of images in the worship of
" God, I cannot but admire at the confi-
" dence of these men, to make so bold a
" charge against them in general, when the
" images of the cherubim were command-
" ed by God himself, Exod. xxv. 22.—
" They were the most solemn and sacred
" part of the Jewish religion; and there-
" fore, though images, so far from idola-
" try, that God made them the seat of his
" presence, and from between them deli-
" vered his oracles; so that something more
" is required to make idolatry, than the
" use of images. This instance is so plain
" and obvious to every reader, there being
" nothing more remarkable in the Old
" Testament, than the honour done to the
" cherubim, that it is a much greater
" wonder to me, that those men who ad-
" vance the objection of idolatry so ground-
" lessly, can so slightly rid themselves of so
" pregnant a proof against it." Ib. pag.

129, 130. And again he says, "Till therefore it be proved that they worship images of false Gods, as the supreme Deities, or that they worship the true God by corporeal images, and representations of his divine nature, there is no footing for idolatry in Christendom." Ib. page 133.

He goes on—"As for the adoration of the host, when they can prove it is given to it, either as a symbol of a false God, or the picture of the true one, howsoever faulty it may be otherwise, it can be no idolatry. And as for the invocation of saints, unless they worship them as the supreme God, the charge of idolatry is an idle word, and the adoration itself that is given to them as saints, is a direct protestation against idolatry, because it supposes a superior deity, and that supposition cuts off the very being of idolatry." Thus far these learned writers, and eminent persons of the Church of England, excuse us from being guilty of what the weak unthinking bulk of Protestants accuse us of; therefore it will be needless to cite any other writers on this subject, and so I shall conclude it, begging the Almighty to dispel that mist which hangs over the eyes of most Protestants, so that
they

they may see things as they really are, and not as vile men paint them.

Proteſtants aſk, By what authority the Roman Catholick Church condemns all others for Hereticks, who do not believe as ſhe teaches, and who gave her that authority?

To this I ſhall give for anſwer a quotation from A Sparrow, Lord Biſhop of Exeter's Collection of Articles, &c. of the Church of England, who in his preface has the following words, "That the church may preſerve herſelf in this purity without ſpot, and in this unity without diviſion, and continue one holy church, as it is in our creed, a double power and authority is needful, as to all bodies politic, ſo likewiſe to this ſociety of believers, the church; one of juriſdiction to correct and reform thoſe impure members, by ſpiritual cenſures, whom counſel will not win, and if they be incorrigible, to caſt them out of this holy ſociety, leſt their leaven ſhould leaven the whole lump, 1 Cor. v. 6.

Thus to preſerve the churches purity, and again to correct and reduce to unity the contentious troublers of the churches peace, if it may be by charitable admonitions, if not to ſtop their mouths, Titus i. 11; not by arguments alone, for ſuch will never prevail upon abſurd, unreaſonable, and obſtinate men, (and such there always will be) but by spiritual censures, even to the casting them out of the churches society, so to preserve peace and unity. Besides this power of jurisdiction, there is necessary also for the obtaining those two high ends, a legislative power to make canons and constitutions upon emergent occasions. For though our great Lord hath already given to his church most holy and wise rules and laws for the same purposes; yet because they are general, not descending to every particularity of time, place, and manner of performance, which yet are necessary to be determined for the preservation of public peace and unity; and because there may, at least through the perverseness of men of corrupt minds, arise some doubts and controversies about the sense and meaning of those most holy rules of our Lord, for the determining of which we are not now to expect any resolution from prophet or oracle, or other immediate voice from Heaven; it doth hereupon necessarily follow, that there must be authority left to this church, and the governors thereof, to make new laws upon these emergent occasions, to determine these particularities, to decide and compose these controversies, whereby to preserve the unity of the Spirit, in the bond of peace. Whosoever shall think that all

this

this may be done by friendly perfuafion, or learned difputes only, will find himfelf deceived, as experience of all ages hath fhewn, and will fhew as long as there be men of perverfe minds, and corrupt affections. Without a definitive and authoritative fentence, controverfies will be endlefs, and the church's peace unavoidably difturbed, and therefore the voice of God and right reafon hath taught, that in matters of controverfy the definitive fentence of fuperiors fhould decide the doubt; and whofoever fhould decline from that fentence, and do prefumptuoufly, fhould be put to death, that others might hear and fear, and do no more prefumptuoufly, Deut. xvii. which is to be underftood myftically alfo of death fpiritual by excommunication, by being cut off from the living body of Chrift's Church.

It being thus cleared by reafon and God's own rule, that fuch power is neceffary for the preferving peace and unity, it cannot be imagined with reafon, that our great Mafter fhould deny his dear bought body fuch neceffaries. But not to reft upon the reafon why they fhould be given; it may be made to appear, that *de facto* he hath given fuch power to the church, and that by reciting his gracious commiffion granted to the church, with his Apoftles practice

and

and exercise of those powers, who best knowing their Lord's will and pleasure, must be, by their practice, the best interpreters of his mind and meaning. See, then, how read we? For the power of jurisdiction, we find a large commission, St. John xx. As my Father sent me, so send I you; and one particular of jurisdiction there expressed, whosoever sins you bind in earth, they are bound in Heaven; a sharp and dreadful sentence, worse than that of the sword, by so much as the death of the soul is worse than the death of the body, which in obstinate despisers of that correction doth too certainly follow.

This power of spiritual censures, St. Paul calls the *rod of discipline*, 1 Cor. iv. ult.— By virtue of this power and commission, St. Paul delivers the incestous Corinthian to Satan, and casts him out of the churches communion, 1 Cor. v. And the same St. Paul not only exercises this jurisdiction himself, but also directs his son, Bishop Timothy, how to behave himself in the ordering the church censures, 1 Tim. v. 19. not to receive an accusation against a Presbyter under two or three witnesses, and when he had heard, to rebuke or censure as the cause requires, without partiality or leaning to either side: all which speak plainly a tribunal erected in the church and ac-

know-

knowledged by the Apostle, enough to prove the power of jurisdiction. Then, the legiflative of making laws and constitutions for regulating manners, and determining doubts and controversies, it cannot with any reason be denied to be granted in this large commission forecited, St. John xx. *As my Father sent me, so send I you.* For here committing the government of the church to his Apostles, our Lord commissions them with the same power that was committed to him for that purpose when he was on earth, with the same necessary standing power that he had and exercised as man for the good of the church; less cannot in reason be thought to be here granted, than all power necessary for the well and peaceable government of the church; and such a power is this of making laws: then in particular for making articles, and decisions of of doctrines controverted, the power is more explicit and express, St. Matt. xxviii. *All power is given to me; go, therefore, and teach all nations,* that is, with authority, and by virtue of that power that is given to me: and what is it to teach the truth with authority, but to command and oblige all people to receive the truth so taught? And this power was not given to the Apostles' persons only, for Christ there promised to be with them in that office to the end of the

the world. This will appear still more clear by St. Paul, Heb. xiii. where after he had commanded them not to be carried about with divers and strange doctrines, he prescribes this as the preservative against such errors and inconstancy, *Obey them that have the sovereignty over you, and watch for your souls*; obey them in the guidance and conduct of your souls, in their determinations and decisions about such divers and strange doctrine, all which supposes in those guides a power to govern and rule us in such doubts and controversies about doctrines and matters of belief; an *authority to determine in controversies of faith*, as our church teaches us in her twentieth *article*: add to this, that St. Paul tells us, 1 Tim. iii. 15. that the church is the *ground and pillar of truth*. And whither, then, should we go in doubts and controversies, for the determination of what is truth? For the clearer understanding of this power in the church, know, that to this *one holy church*, our Lord committed in trust the most holy faith, and the whole stock of necessary Christian truth, therefore called the ground and pillar of truth."

Thus far this Protestant Bishop—And from him any person may see, that hath eyes, by what authority all Hereticks are condemned, and also who gave the church

that

that authority to condemn such disturbers of her unity. Yea, from what this Bishop has said, all Protestants may understand, on what a weak foundation their so much boasted reformation is built; for if the church has the power which this Bishop proves she has, I then ask, what lawful power had Luther, or Calvin, or any of the first Reformers to censure and condemn the Sacraments and rites of the Roman Catholic Church? Yea, I want to know what power could oblige her to submit herself to be judged by any private man?

Now Luther and Calvin were both private men, and bred up in her communion, therefore could have no lawful commission, or authority, but what they received from her; and after the church had cut off from her holy society, these disturbers of her unity, what other holy church authorised them to preach up their two contrary faiths? for Luther preached up contrary to Calvin, and Calvin contrary to Luther, and each one anathemised the other and his followers; and the Church of England faith is contrary to both: and so does every reformed church differ from all others that ever were before them, for which reason all of them cannot be of God, because God is not the author of confusion, but of unity.

As the Church of England glories in allowing her adversaries the freedom of an impartial examination of her doctrine and religion, I hope, ~~that~~ as I have answered many questions, that none of her Pastors will be offended at me for asking the following *plain* ones:

I. *Whether the Church of England joined in communion unto any church that always had a being, and was always a visible and known society of christians, from our Saviour's time, and what nation it was in?* For if she did not join herself unto the true and universal Church of Christ, she must be a *new sect*.

II. *Whether the Church of England be the Apostolic Church of Christ, or not?* For except her Ministers can shew that she be in communion with the Catholic Church, which the Apostles built, and which has in her a continued succession of Pastors and doctrine from them to the present time, they must own that she is an *upstart*, and *New Church*.

III. *Whether the Protestant Church can be the Catholic Church of all ages, when the very name of Protestant was utterly unknown till after the year* 1519? And if she be not Catholic, she must be a *new sect*.

IV. *Whether laity, clergy, learned and unlearned, all ages, sects and degrees of men, women and children, in whole Christendom,*

were

*were drowned in abominable idolatry, for the space of* 800 *years, and more, as the Homily against peril of idolatry expresses it?* If they were not, the Homily teaches falsities, and so do the Articles of the Church of England: for the 35th Article approves the said Homily, as containing (with others of the like kind) good and wholesome doctrine, and necessary for these times.

V. *Whether the Church of England must not have received her authority to preach and administer the Sacraments from abominable idolaters?* Because, according to her own doctrine, there was none but such in whole Christendom for 800 years and more before her time; therefore, if none of the Apostles came down from Heaven to authorise and ordain her Ministers, she must be an *idolatrous church:* because she could not (as she herself teaches) receive ordination or authority from *any other*, every age, sect, and human creature, as says the Homily, being overwhelmed in *abominable idolatry.*

VI. *Whether, if the aforesaid Homily be true, the scripture and Creeds be not false?* For if the scripture be true, Christ always had a church, such as it describes the same to be, namely, *the pillar and support of truth,* always orthodox, always visible; always known, and always spread over the earth. And if the creeds be true, Christ had, in the ages immediately before the Reformation, *one holy, catholic* (that is universal, orthodox) *and apostolic church, the communion of Saints;* therefore, it is plain, that either the Homily must be false, or else the holy scripture and creed are.

VII. *Whether the true service of God had been corrupted throughout the whole world before King Edward's time?* Or if not, tell me where was the Province upon earth that it did exist in?

VIII. *Whether at this day there be no pure and apostolical service of God in the world, except that established by law, in England and Ireland?*

IX. *Whether it be lawful for the people of England to invent a church to themselves, divided from all the rest of the Christian world?*

X. *Whether the Church of England be not changeable according to the various inclinations of English Parliaments?*

XI. Whether the 39 Articles of the Church of England, be articles of faith; yea, or no? If they are not, then nobody is bound to believe them,; if they be, then hath the Church of England invented new articles of faith, besides those twelve instituted by Christ and his Apostles.

XII. Whether that be a true church which wants lawful pastors? And whether
pastors

pastors not lawful and true, can be said to administer true Sacraments? If not, then is it not better to communicate with Catholics under one kind, than with Protestants under no kind?

XIII. Whether want of mission be not an error in the foundation of any church? It being theft and robbery (as our Saviour hath taught us) not to enter by the door into the sheepfold.

XIV. Whether Queen Elizabeth's Bishops entered by the Parliament door, or by a lawful succession from the Apostles? For none less than a Bishop, can consecrate another Bishop, by reason, no man can lawfully give to another, what he is not lawfully in possession of himself.

XV. Whether the bible does not admit of various interpretations? And if so, whether some judge is not to be assigned to determine which is the true interpretation? For if there is to be no judge in this case, people may wrangle for ever, and one say the scripture means so, and another not so, even to the world's end.

Observe, the present Protestants build their faith upon the bible that was translated in King James's time, but the Protestants before that time built upon the bible translated in Queen Elizabeth's time, and those before

before her time, took that tranflated by Tindal, to be the infallible word of God.

The Proteftants abroad, fome believe Luther's tranflation to be the infallible rule which they ought to go by; others take Beza's tranflation; others prefer Zuinglius's tranflation; and others Oecolampadius's; others Caftalio's; and all think themfelves certain of having the true and infallible word of God, and yet, to their eternal confufion, all condemn each other, and expofe the falfities of one another's tranflations; as hear from their own mouths.

Firft, concerning Luther's tranflation, hear what the great Zuinglius fays, in his Lib. de Sacra. fol. 412. " Luther was
" (fays he) a foul corrupter, and horrible
" falfifier of God's word: one who follow-
" ed the Marcionifts and Arians, that ra-
" zed out fuch places of holy writ as were
" againft him. Thou doft, (fays he to Lu-
" ther) corrupt the word of God, thou art
" feen to be a manifeft and common cor-
" rupter and perverter of the holy fcrip-
" tures. How much are we afhamed of
" thee, who have hitherto efteemed thee."
&c.

When Zuinglius had printed his bible at Zurich, the printer fent one to Luther, but he rejected it, and fent it back again; as fee in the Proteftants Apoligie Tract. 1. S. 10.

Subd.

Subd. 4. saying, "that the translators were fools, asses, antichrists, deceivers, and of an ass like understanding."

When Oecolampadius had set forth his bible at Basil, Beza said thus of it, "The Basilian translation is in many places wicked, and altogether differing from the mind of the Holy Ghost."

The same great Beza accounts that so highly esteemed translation of Castalio, "to be sacrilegious, wicked, and ethnical." And in his annotations calls it, "false, foolish, unskilful, bold, blasphemous, vicious, ridiculous, cursed, erroneous, wicked and perverse."

Castalio wrote a whole book against Beza's translation, and said, "That to note all his errors (in translating) would require a great volume." Here you see these translations of your prime doctors, condemned by the authority of others, no less famous translators; and both those who were condemned thus, and who did thus condemn, were men more famous among you, than any one translator of any one English bible. And if these learned translations were so full of corruptions, how can you hope that your English translators have done their parts better than any of these great doctors. Therefore, your building your faith on the bible, as translated

in

in England, cannot be an infallible faith, and without an infallible rule of faith, none can be saved.

Now hear what has been said against the English translators, by English Protestants.

Upon Queen Elizabeth's making three articles, to be subscribed by all her clergy, one of which was, that the book of common prayer contains nothing contrary to the word of God.

Divers ministers, in a treatise to her excellent Majesty, spoke thus, " Our trans-
" lation of the psalms, comprized in our
" book of common prayer, does, in additi-
" on, substraction, and alteration, differ
" from the truth of the Hebrew, in two
" hundred places, at least."

And Mr. Burges, in his Apology, S. 6. writes thus, " How shall I approve, under
" my hand, a translation which has many
" omissions, many additions, which some-
" times obscures, sometimes perverts the
" sense, being sometimes senseless, sometimes
" contrary."

And Carlial faith, in his book of Christ's descent into Hell, p. 116. " The trans-
" lators thereof (the English bible) have
" depraved the sense, or obscured the truth,
" and deceived the ignorant. In many
" places they detort the scripture from the

right

"right sense; and finally, they shew them-
"selves to love darkness more than light,
"falshood more than truth."

When King James came in, the Ministers of Lincolnshire, in an abridgment of a book delivered to the King. p. 11, 12, of the English translation speak thus, "It takes "away from the text, adds to the text, and "this sometimes to the changing or obscur- "ing of the meaning of the Holy Ghost."

Dr. Reynolds, in a meeting of Bishops, at Hampton-Court, mentioned, That there might be a new translation of the Bible, because the present translations were corrupt and not answerable to the truth of the original: and after King James's Bible was printed, Mr. Broughton (a man as skilful in Hebrew and Greek as any was in England) did give this censure in his advertisements of corruptions to the Bishops; saying, "That their public translation of the "scriptures into English, is such, that it "perverteth the text of the Old Testa- "ment in 848 places, and that it causeth "millions to reject the New Testament, "and to run into eternal flames."

You are also to observe, that in Queen Elizabeth's time to the last day of her reign, her clergy subscribed that the false Bible which they then had, was the true word of God; though it is now proved to be quite contrary (in many places) to the true word of God. The scripture which they then had was held to be the only rule of faith, and cited as fast, and as thick for God's word then, as it is now: and yet the present Bible tells us fairly that the other was not God's true word, but false words, of false translators.

And pray, what comfort can any Protestant have who is obliged to rely on what his present translators say, and to take that for his only divine rule of faith which they have thought proper to alter as best suited with their purpose? to give a few instances of their disingenuity, I will cite a translation of the 18th chapter of St. Luke, and the 42d verse, where the present translation says, " Thy faith hath saved thee," in place of saying, " Thy faith hath made thee whole." And in Matt. xix. 11. the translator makes Christ tell us, " All men cannot receive " this saying;" whereas Christ said only, " All men do not receive this saying," as is evident out of the Greek

Now when translators make no conscience of wilfully falsifying God's own word, in favour of their own opinions, I may justly say, that protestants cannot be sure of their faith in all points; because they take a false translation as the only rule of faith in all points:

points: wherefore it is neceſſary, for all thoſe who wiſh to gain Heaven, to build their faith on a more ſure foundation, ſuch as is the church, which is the foundation, or pillar and ſupport of truth itſelf. And I aſk, who can find half ſo ſure a ground to build their faith upon, as is the church, which St. Paul affirms to be the pillar and ground of truth?

XVI. Whether religion be ſacred if eſtabliſhed by the laws of the land? If it be, why did Queen Elizabeth deſtroy the Catholic religion which had been eſtabliſhed by a number of laws, even for ages before her time?

XVII. Whether it is not more ſafe to die in the old faſhion religion of our Catholic anceſtors, who derived their miniſterial order from the very Apoſtles themſelves, than in any new faith ſprung up ſince the year of our Lord 1500, yea, though they ſhould have their power and authority from the Parliament itſelf? If to die in the former is ſafeſt, by reaſon old Chriſtian faiths are beſt, then let each ſtand in the way of his old Catholic anceſtors, and ſeek after the goodly paths in which they trod, and walk therein. For the marks of hereſy, are the new faiths it teaches, therefore avoid all novelties in religion, becauſe there is but one Ca-

tholic

tholic Church, in which alone is the communion of Saints.

XVIII. Whether Christ did not command all men to obey his church under pain of being looked upon as excommunicated persons? And if so, whether it was the Church of England that he taught us to obey, or whether it was not the holy Catholic Church, in which is the communion of Saints, unto whom we owe obedience? If it was the former, then I would ask, Unto what church obedience was due before the present Church of England had a *name or being?* For the command was given upwards of 1500 years before the words *Protestant Church*, were so much as *known*, or *heard of*. Besides, I ask, In what country or nation did the church exist in, unto whom we ought to pay obedience? but if it is the holy Catholic Church alone, which we are obliged to obey, even in matters of private quarrels, as well as those of points of faith; I then ask, Whether the Church of England could separate herself from her faith and communion without being guilty of heresy?

XIX. Whether the holy Catholic Church can err in settling points of faith, yea, or no? If she cannot, then it is plain she is infallible: and if she can *err* then she ceases to be *holy*; and in consequence, the creeds
cease

cease to be true; therefore if the creeds be true, there always was a *holy and unerring Church*.

XX. Whether a Protestant, professing before God and man that he believes in one holy Catholick Church, and at the same time acknowledging that it is impossible for any church to be holy, does not profess to believe a gross contradiction? For if he is positive that no church upon earth can be free from error, because composed of falible men, then he cannot mean what his words express in the creeds: for to be *holy*, is to be free from *error*; therefore, whatever church it is that errs in points of faith, she is not the *holy Catholic Church of Christ*, but the church of some *Heretic* who imposed on the credulity of men.

XXI. I ask, Whether the Church of England Bishops at their first beginning, were directed by the Holy Ghost in the making their faith, or not? If they were not, then the church which they established was not the church of Christ, for Christ promised that the Holy Ghost should abide with his church for ever, to guide and direct her into all truth.

If it is answered, that they were directed by the Holy Ghost, then I ask, whether any man, or set of men, could presume to alter the faith and articles which they first made,

without

without being guilty of herefy or fchifm? Becaufe whatever the Holy Ghoft dictates will always remain truth, and never can need altering.

But at the firft eftablifhing the reformed church of England, auricular confeffion was retained, and the whole high mafs, with thefe alterations only, namely, That there fhould be but two lights upon the high altar, that the Epiftles and Gofpels fhould be read in Englifh and not in Latin, that the Prieft fhould confecrate more wine than ufual, and not drink all up himfelf, and that every of the breads fhould be broke into two, or more pieces. Now if the Holy Ghoft directed the firft eftablifhers of the Church of England's faith, (as they boaftingly faid he did) to retain the mafs and auricular confeffion; I then afk, what fpirit directed the abolifhing them, as they are now at this day?

The fame Holy Spirit could not, becaufe whatever the Holy Ghoft dictates are eternal truths, and can never need mending; and if the Holy Ghoft did not direct the abolifhing the mafs and auricular confeffion, then the prefent faith of the Church of England muft be wrong.

Therefore either the bleffed Reformers (as they called themfelves) were wrong at their firft fetting off, or elfe the prefent

Church

Church of England is so now; and if the first glorious Reformers were impostors, and not sent by God to teach his truths; what is to be thought of the present Church of England who sprung from them, and is a branch of the same tree? Christ himself having told us, that a corrupt tree cannot bring forth good fruit, neither can a good tree bring forth corrupt fruit. Now if the present pastors of the Church of England cannot clear the first Reformers from being guilty of teaching errors in points of faith, then their own faith must be looked upon as built on a weak and sandy foundation.

*Note*, The statute that enacted the mass to be retained, says, (2 and 3 Edward VIth, c. 1.) " Was made by the Archbishop of
" Canterbury, and certain of the most learn-
" ed and discreet Bishops, and other learn-
" ed men of this realm, having as well
" eye and respect to the most sincere and
" pure Christian religion taught in scrip-
" ture, as to the primitive church; and was
" by the aid of the Holy Ghost, with one
" agreement, concluded, set forth, and de-
" livered to his Majesty, to his great com-
" fort and quiet of mind," *who was then about twelve years old, and no doubt, must be thought a very fit person to be the supreme Head and Director of Christ's Church, and able to judge as well as some others how it*

*ought*

*ought to be patched and mended.* And yet when he came to be about three years older, the mass, which had given him such great comfort and quiet of mind, was laid aside, and another liturgy introduced, although the very statute that disanulled the former, says, (5 and 6 Edward VIth, c. 1.) that it was *a very godly order, agreeable to the word of God, and the primitive Church, very comfortable to all good people desiring to live in Christian conversation, and most profitable to the estate of this realm.* And after, it says, *That the doubts in the use and exercise of it, were rather by the curiosity of Ministers, and mistakes, than of any other worldly cause.*—Strange, that it should need altering!

XXII. Whether the rule of faith which all new churches build upon, of interpreting scripture by their own private judgment, or by the private spirit of their new teachers, be the true rule of Christian faith?

XXIII. Whether the members of any new religion are certain that any private interpreter understands the true meaning of the scripture, as the Holy Ghost intended it to be understood? For if their private interpreters do not, they have no true divine faith.

XXIV. Whether a private interpretation of scripture be not mere human opinion, and only the words of the interpreter suggested by by his own spirit, and if so, how can it be the infallible word of God?

XXV. Whether he who pretends to interpret scripture by his own private judgmen, is not in danger of fathering the extravagant productions of his own brain on the word of God?

XXVI. Whether the true ministers of Christ can be any other than such as come down by succession from the Apostles of Christ? If they cannot, it is then plain that the teachers of all new sects are not the true ministers of Christ, and therefore have no power, or commission to bless in his name, or to preach his word, or to administer his sacraments, because they do not come down in a regular succession from the Apostles of Christ, neither were they ever licenced or impowered by the pastors of the Church of Christ who had authority handed down to them from the Apostles, who were originally commissioned by Christ himself, who said, *As my Father sent me, I send you*, St. John xx.

And as the teachers of all new sects have no commission from God in the ordinary way, as the pastors of Christ's Church ought to have, I then ask,

Whether they have any extraordinary commission immediately from God himself? If they say they have, I then ask them to
produce

produce their proper credentials, as Moses and the Apostles did; that is, I ask them to shew one evident miracle worked by them in proof of their being the extraordinary Delegates of God? And if they cannot give these proofs, then it is plain they never were sent by God in this manner, therefore must be wolves in sheep's cloathing, of whom all men ought to beware, notwithstanding *their boasting of the Spirit*, their outward *shew of Religion*, their *formal cant*, larded with *texts of Scripture*, wrested to serve *a turn*, and their crying out *Lord, Lord*, though the Lord never sent them, *neither is his truth amongst them.*

XXVII. Whether any of the Protestant Religions be the true Religion, which was taught by Christ and his Apostles, and which it is that has that antiquity on its side? For if any of them was taught by Christ, it then will follow, that the Protestant Religion had a being before Popery, and that there was a change from Protestancy to Popery—I then ask,

XXVIII. Whether any one can tell the time when Popery came into the world, and who were the first broachers of it, and what authentic history can be produced which has been handed down to posterity, which shews when this change of Religion happened?

XXIX. I

XXIX. I aſk, who were the firſt inventors or promoters of the maſs, and what was the names of thoſe zealous Proteſtant Biſhops who wrote againſt it at its firſt appearance?

XXX. I alſo aſk, who was the firſt Pope, Biſhop, or Prieſt who ſaid maſs, and what reſiſtance he met with, and what councils condemned it: and ſhould alſo be glad to know with what reluctance people were at firſt brought to be preſent at it, and whether the whole Chriſtian world was bribed, or bullied into it, for before Luther's time, all the Prieſts and Biſhops in the world ſaid maſs? Now if theſe queſtions cannot be anſwered clearly, this will prove the Religion of the Church of Rome as ancient as Chriſtianity itſelf; becauſe we can ſhew the very time when any ſect aroſe, and who oppoſed it, when it was condemned, and what diſturbances it raiſed; and can produce authentic records, when any hereſy was firſt broached, and who were the broachers of it, and who oppoſed it, &c. therefore, if Proteſtants cannot do the like, concerning Popery, it will then be evident that Popery was the firſt Religion; and, in conſequence, the very ſame which was taught by Chriſt and his Apoſtles; and whether it ought to be followed or not, I will leave every thinking person, who hopes to gain a happy eternity, to judge for himself, humbly concluding with hoping that it is not impossible, but that the once great and glorious *Britain* may awake from her long lethargy, may cease to fight against Heaven, may not oppose her own safety, nor shut the gate against her own happiness.

Oh, my countrymen! where is the glory of your Catholic ancestors, which heretofore made this Island looked upon as a *land of benediction*, which opened her liberal breasts to give *so many Doctors* to Europe, *so many lights of learning to the Church, so many examples of piety to Christendom,* and so many *Confessors to Paradise?* Your kings by a pious violence have forced their way to Heaven, and their people have followed their footsteps. There was nothing spoken of this happy country, but *their obedience to the Church, their piety, their virtue,* and *their constancy;* but since the Devil of *lust* and *rebellion,* raised from the most black abyss, hath seized on the soul of miserable King Henry the VIIIth, whose long reign seemed to be given him (as to Herod, and Tiberius, and other tyrants) to fill up the measure of his iniquity; you have sullied your *perfection,* you have destroyed your *sanctuary,* the lamentable *relicks* whereof are now spread over all the *world,* and the sacred stones of
your

your temples groaning amongst the nations, do attend the day of the justice of God, and the re-union of all your hearts in the performance of his service. What have you done with the precious relicks of those *holy saints and martyrs,* which this happy soil claimed for her offspring, whose virtuous lives filled the world with *admiration?*

*Return, O Shunamite; return, return,* fair Island, to thy first beginning.— The hand of God is not shortened, his arms all day are *stretched forth to receive thee!* If the insolent hands of heresy have made them bars, which have encompassed thee many years, do not think but the hands of true piety will tear away the disorders which protect themselves in *the night of so corrupted an age.* Fright not yourselves at imaginary horrors, and overthrowings of estates by the inquisitions and thunders of Rome: for these are all mere bugbears to affright the timorous; the beams of religious truths will bring forth *joy, love, peace, and happiness;* and if you persevere in goodness, you may expect such glorious effects that *you yourselves cannot believe, nor your posterity sufficiently admire.*

Oh my dear *Britons,* put on once more the yoke of Christ, *for it is easy, and his burden*

*burden is light*, and perform the pious and virtuous actions of your Catholic anceſtors. Oh! for the love of your own ſouls, embrace that religion which they practiſed by *their virtues*, demonſtrated by *their examples*, honoured by *their conſtancy*, and which many ſealed with *their blood*.

THE END.

www.ingramcontent.com/pod-product-compliance
Lightning Source LLC
Chambersburg PA
CBHW020826230426
43666CB00007B/1118